ALBERTO SILIOTTI

GUIDE TO EXPLORAT

— OF THE —

SINAI

SWAN·HILL
PRESS

GUIDE TO EXPLORATION
OF THE
SINAI

Text
Alberto Siliotti

Editorial Supervision by
Valeria Manferto De Fabianis
Laura Accomazzo

Illustrations by
Cristina Franco

Cartographic and architectural survey
Yvonne Marzoni di Cossato, Alberto Siliotti,
Claudio Concina

Graphic Supervision by
Patrizia Balocco Lovisetti

Translation by
Antony Shugaar

© 1994 White Star S.r.l. Via Candido Sassone, 24
Vercelli, Italy.

First Published in the UK in 1996 by Swan Hill Press,
an imprint of Airlife Publishing Ltd.

British Library
Cataloguing in Publication Data
A catalogue record for this book is available from the
British Library

ISBN 1 85310 796 4

All rights reserved. No part of this book may be reproduced
or transmitted in any form or by any means, electronic or
mechanical including photocopying, recording or by any
information storage and retrieval system, without
permission from the Publisher in writing.

Printed in Italy by Grafedit Bergamo, Italy.
Colour separations by Fotolito Star, Bergamo, Italy.

SWAN HILL PRESS
an imprint of Airlife Publishing Ltd.
101 Longden Road, Shrewsbury SY3 9EB, England

The publisher
would like to thank
Giorgia Facchinelli
for her valuable
assistance in the
writing of this book

Contents

INTRODUCTION   page   6

NORTHERN SINAI   page   22
- From the Suez Canal to el-Arish   page   22
- Pelusium, the "Gate of Egypt"   page   23
- From el-Arish to the Suez Canal   page   25

WEST COAST OF THE SINAI   page   26
- Tunnel A.H. — El Tor — Sharm el-Sheikh   page   26
- The temple of Serabit and the turquoise deposits   page   31
- The Region of Serabit El Khadem — Bir Nasib   page   31
- Wadi Feiran   page   38
- Wadi Mukattab — Wadi Maghara — Gebel Fuga   page   40
- Ras Mohammed   page   43

SHARM EL-SHEIKH   page   61
- Wadi el-Aat   page   72
- Wadi Mandar   page   75
- Wadi Kid — Oasis of Ain Kid   page   76
- National Park of Nabq — Oasis of
  the Mangroves — Wadi Qabila   page   78

STRAIT OF TIRAN   page   82

FROM NAAMA BAY TO DAHAB   page   86
- Wadi Madsus — Wadi Shetan — Wadi
  Shellal — Wadi Nasb — Oasis of Nasb   page   88

DAHAB   page   91
- Wadi Qnai el-Rayan   page   92
- Wadi Qnai el-Atshan   page   92
- Wadi Connection — Rest Valley Mountain   page   94
- Dahab — Blue Hole   page   96

DAHAB-NUWEIBA-TABA   page   100
- Dahab — Nuweiba — Saint Catherine   page   104
- Natural Park of Abu Galum   page   108
- Track from Nuweiba to Ain Khudra   page   112
- Colored Canyon   page   114
- Oasis of Ain Umm Ashmed   page   118

SAINT CATHERINE   page   120
- The Monastery   page   122
- Gebel Musa   page   138
- Saint Catherine — Galt el-Azraq   page   146
- Gebel Katherina   page   150
- The Blue Desert   page   152

GLOSSARY   page   155
USEFULL NUMBERS   page   155
INDEX OF LOCALITIES   page   157

*1 In this general
view of the
promontory of Ras
Mohammed it is
possible to see, on
the left, the Island of
the Mangroves and
the nearby canal,
and on the right,
the Shark
Observatory.*

*2 The monastery of
St. Catherine, located
in the center of the
Sinai peninsula and
built upon the site
where tradition has
it that Moses saw the
Burning Bush, has
been a destination
for pilgrims for more
than fifteen centuries.*

*4-5 This satellite
photograph shows
the Sinai peninsula,
framed between the
Gulf of Suez and
the Gulf of Aqaba.*

INTRODUCTION

The Sinai peninsula - which is believed to take its name from an ancient lunar deity called Sin, although that origin is sometimes questioned - juts out into the Red Sea, sandwiched between the Gulf of Suez and the Gulf of Eilat.
The Sinai desert is considered to be the third largest in Egypt (ranked behind the Libyan desert to the west of the Nile and the Arabian desert to the Nile's east). This territory, rich in mineral deposits of great value, such as copper and turquoise, was the destination of continual expeditions beginning at the time of Egypt's Old Kingdom; these expeditions endured long voyages in order to obtain Sinai's precious raw materials. A thousand years later, according to tradition, the events narrated in the Bible, in Exodus, occurred in the desert and on the mountain tops of the Sinai. Here Moses is said to have received the Ten Commandments,

here the Hebrews made their painful way along the road to the Promised Land, one of the holiest destinations for pilgrims of the Christian and the Jewish faiths. The mountains of the Sinai culminate in Mount Saint Catherine, or Gebel Katherina, and in the Mount of Moses, or Gebel Musa, behind which stands the renowned convent of Saint Catherine.
They occupy the south central portion of the Sinai peninsula and then run gradually down to the crystal clear waters of the Red Sea. Here, in a pristine sea, one can admire an abundance of fish of all species and teeming in numbers, perhaps among the richest in the world. Desert and sea are the two elements that predominate in the Sinai; often desert and sea meet, creating panoramas and settings that are unrivalled in grandeur and in exquisite beauty.

GEOLOGY OF THE SINAI

Some familiarity with the long geological history of the Sinai peninsula if one wishes to understand, interpret, and appreciate the remarkable views and landscapes of this land - in appearance, harsh and desert, but in reality one of the richest site for naturalists in the world today - as well as a vast array of very interesting geological phenomena. The Sinai's geological history has, in fact, greatly affected the peninsula's physical appearance and geography, its fauna and its flora, and the people that have settled and lived here over the millennia. A thorough analysis of the complex geological structure of the Sinai peninsula would require a great deal of space and would completely subvert the original purpose of this guide; we are therefore obliged to omit a great deal of detail and to simplify our presentation of this interesting topic, so as to provide the reader with the concise information necessary to a basic understanding of the landscape here. In the Sinai, it is possible to distinguish by and large among three areas that differ radically one from another.
The first area lies to the north and consists of sand dunes and quaternarian deposits. These deposits correspond to the sites of ancient wadis (this word is used to describe river beds which tend to be fossil streams, although they may become active from time to time) and fossil beaches that were formed by the changing level of the Mediterranean Sea during the glacial and interglacial periods that so typified the Quaternary Period that began about two million years ago. This area is fairly homogeneous, and consists of a rather flat and uniform landscape that is broken up toward the south by a series of vast rock islets; these rocks correspond to the limestone of the Cretaceous Period (which would date from about sixty million years ago). The desert is also broken by the vast and magnificent hulk of the Gebel Maghara, made up of even more ancient limestone and sandstone of the Jurassic

6 The triangular shape of the Sinai peninsula stands out sharply against the surface of the sea. Because of its tectonic origins, which is to say,

because of the spreading movements of the great continental plates, the Gulf of Eilat is far deeper than the Gulf of Suez.

7 top left The Sinai is crisscrossed by a dense welter of wadis, an Arab word that indicates the valleys formed by ancient watercourses, dried out.

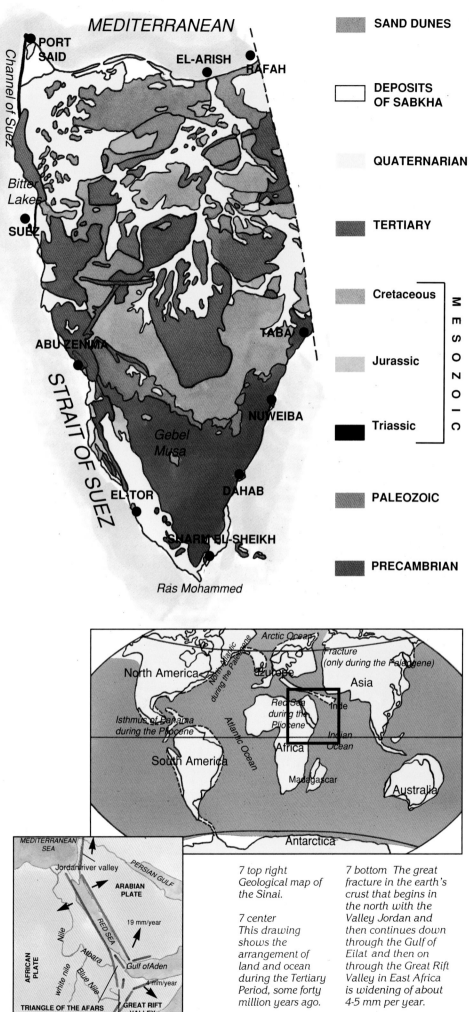

Period. To the south of the mountainous system of the Gebel Maghara the second area begins, occupying the central portion of the Sinai peninsula; here the quaternarian formations are broken up by the numerous and extensive outcroppings of limestone dating from the Tertiary Period (generally from the Eocene epoch and rarely from the Paleocene) which also make up the immense highland of el-Tih, the true geographic center of the Sinai peninsula. This highland extends toward the south and is surrounded by a constellation of other limestone outcroppings from the Cretaceous; these separate the highland from an area of granitic and volcanic rock. This is the third of the areas into which we have divided the Sinai peninsula. Here the landscape changes radically and abruptly; the variegated sandstone and limestone is replaced by two types of rock - granite and basalt - that are both magmatic, in contrast with the two previous types, limestone and sandstone, which are sedimentary in nature. Basalts are both effusive rocks, which means that they are produced by volcanic activity on the bottom of the ocean. The volcanic zone is, in turn, bounded - especially to the west - by extensive outcroppings of quaternarian rock that correspond to ancient coral formations that also form the southernmost tip of the peninsula.

SAND DUNES

DEPOSITS OF SABKHA

QUATERNARIAN

TERTIARY

Cretaceous

Jurassic

Triassic

M E S O Z O I C

PALEOZOIC

PRECAMBRIAN

7 top right
Geological map of the Sinai.

7 center
This drawing shows the arrangement of land and ocean during the Tertiary Period, some forty million years ago.

7 bottom The great fracture in the earth's crust that begins in the north with the Valley Jordan and then continues down through the Gulf of Eilat and then on through the Great Rift Valley in East Africa is widening of about 4-5 mm per year.

THE MINES OF THE PHARAOHS

The deposits of turquoise and of copper minerals (such as malachite) present in the Sinai (we should also mention vast deposits of flint) attracted peoples who came to settle from both the east and the north. The first migrations occurred specifically in the so-called B preceramic period (around the sixth millennium B.C.). These earliest mining colonizers moved slowly southward, halting their migrations in all the places where minerals were most abundant; evidence of this has been supplied by a number of excavations carried out in Wadi Ahmar, in the region around Saint Catherine,

2920-2575 B.C.) in the northernmost regions; the Egyptians subjugated the peoples of the Timna culture. From the beginning of the Third Dynasty onward, the Egyptians began to send expeditions to the Sinai in order to start systematic mining and quarrying of the mineral deposits in the region: in Wadi Maghara, in fact, a bas relief depicting pharaoh Sekhemkhet has been discovered which can fairly be considered to be one of the earliest indications of the presence of Egyptians in the Sinai. This mining and quarrying activity reached a peak during the Middle Kingdom and continued

8 This picture depicts one of the great turquoise mines, now played out, in the side of Gebel Maghara.

9 left At Serabit el-Khadem — an Arab name that means "mountain of the fortress," located in a region abundant in copper and turquoise mines — a small temple, dedicated to the goddess Hathor, "the lady of turquoise," and the god Sopdu, "Lord of the Foreign Lands," had already been built during the Twelfth Dynasty.

where neolithic arrow points were found, along with slag and residue from the smelting of copper minerals. In the period of the Timna culture (Timna I and Timna II), around 3500 B.C., the mining and smelting of copper flourished greatly and led an increase in the population of the Sinai; these same early settlers were mining turquoise as well, in Serabit el-Khadem. The pharaohs of the first dynasties soon began to express interest in the Sinai, and the earliest colonization took place as early as the Thinite era (circa

subsequently right up to the New Kingdom, with a few interruptions only during the Intermediate Periods: the last name for which we have documentation at Serabit el-Khadem is that of pharaoh Ramesses VI (Twentieth Dynasty), while the last pharaoh during whose reign the working of copper minerals truly flourished was Ramesses III. Nonetheless, the Egyptians never truly colonized the Sinai, and it always remained in their view a harsh and desolate land; they did no more than to send expeditions from time to time and to create labor camps near the sites of the mines and the quarries. Although a labor camp has been uncovered near Wadi Kharig with fragments of crucibles used in smelting dating from the Fifth Dynasty (as is shown by a hieroglyphic inscription dedicated to pharaoh Sahure, carved into a nearby rock), the greatest level of development attained in the extraction of copper and turquoise came under the Twelfth Dynasty, during the reign of Amenemhat III: from this period, in fact, dates an enormous deposit of mineral slag found at Bir Nasib, not far from Serabit el-Khadem. The slag heap is estimated to be about 100,000 tons.

9 top right
This bas-relief, discovered by the English explorer E. H. Palmer in 1868 on the east face of Gebel Maghara, depicts the pharaoh

Sekhemkhet of the Third Dynasty (about 2600 B.C.) and indicates that turquoise was mined in extremely ancient times at Wadi Maghara.

9 center right
Turquoise, a semiprecious stone much sought after during the times of the pharaohs, was first quarried in the Sinai as early as the Old Kingdom, which is to say, during the third millennium B.C.

9 bottom right
During the Eighteenth Dynasty, the temple of Serabit el-Khadem was enlarged considerably, acquiring its modern-day form.

THE HEBREWS, THE EXODUS, AND MOUNT SINAI

The presence of the Hebrews (called *Apirou* in ancient texts) in Egypt has been attested as early as the reign of Tuthmosis III, as well as in the Ramesside period: they worked as stone cutters and stone haulers, masons, carpenters; they also cultivated vineyards. This early documentation is sporadic and haphazard; passages in the Papyrus of Leida 348 or the Harris Papyrus I, tell us that the largest Hebrew community, residing at Madjan, near modern-day Eilat, was completely free and that the Hebrews traded with the Egyptians. The Egyptian sources say nothing about an Exodus, and the only document that mentions the name of Israel is a stele held in the collections of the Cairo Museum, dating from Year Five of the reign of pharaoh Merneptah, the son of Ramesses II. Knowing that the battle of Jericho took place in 1250 B.C. and that the Hebrews wandered in the desert for forty years, we can make a hypothetical conjecture that the great deeds done by Moses in Egypt took place during the reign of Ramesses II, when work was going forward full tilt on the fortifications of the Delta and on the construction of the future city of Pi-Ramesses; we can further conjecture that the Exodus took place during the reign of Merneptah. According to classical sources, the Hebrews set out from the eastern Delta (from Pi-Ramesses or from Pitom), and then set out for the Sinai, crossing the Red Sea (Exodus, 14) at a spot that has not been properly identified geographically; it may have been either Lake Timsah or the southern tip of Lake Manzala or of Lake Bardawil. Later still, the Hebrews moved southward until they reached the "Mountain of God," considered to be the modern-day Gebel Musa. From here they moved on toward Ezion-Gaber and Eilat, and subsequently headed north in the direction of Kadesh-Barnea, which was to become the main base for the Israelis in their conquest of this territory. In reality, it is fairly unlikely that this was actually the route followed in the Exodus. For one thing it makes absolutely no logical sense; for another, it would be exceedingly difficult to make this journey because of the scarcity of water sufficient for such a great a number of people. Scholars have therefore thought of a possible alternative, known as the "northern route," which sets forth a more realistic itinerary, running at first parallel to the Mediterranean coast, and then cutting south toward Gebel Halal and from there Kadesh-Barnea. In this geographic region, therefore, the true Mount Sinai of the Bible is probably located.

10 top
A stand of palm trees stands out in the arid landscape of the Sinai peninsula, contrasting sharply with the hot colors of the sandstone and limestone that make up the surrounding mountains.

10 bottom
For many years, camels constituted the chief means of transportation along the rough, badly marked tracks of the Sinai.

11 top The eastern slope of the Gebel Musa is shown here in all its powerful majesty. On the summit, one can barely glimpse the tiny chapel dedicated to the Holy Trinity.

11 center Aside from the Gebel Musa, other great mountains in the region, such as Gebel Serbal or Gebel Katherina — shown here from Wadi Zawatin — all peaks that rise above two thousand meters (about sixty-five hundred feet), have been indicated as the "true" mountain of God, but ever since the fourth century A.D., monks and hermits have identified Gebel Musa as the mountain upon which God appeared to Moses, and early on chapels and little hermitages were built around this sacred site.

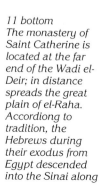

11 bottom The monastery of Saint Catherine is located at the far end of the Wadi el-Deir; in distance spreads the great plain of el-Raha. Accordiong to tradition, the Hebrews during their exodus from Egypt descended into the Sinai along

the coast of the Gulf of Suez, and then climbed up the Wadi Feiran and camped in the plain of el-Raha, where a mountain stood called the Gebel Musa, or Mount of Moses, upon which the patriarch supposedly received the tablets of the Ten Commandments.

CONTEMPORARY HISTORY

In 1979, the President of Egypt, the late Anwar Sadat, and the Prime Minister of Israel, Menachem Begin, signed, in the presence of the President of the United States Jimmy Carter, the so-called Camp David Peace Agreement, putting an end to a prolonged period of hostilities between Egypt and Israel, resulting in the withdrawal of Israeli troops from the Sinai. During this sensitive phase, the United Nations participated as observers and peacekeepers, to ensure the proper application of the treaty. The Sinai was split up into three zones, where the Egyptian military presence had to be limited according to the terms of the agreement; while the same limitations were applied to the zones on the Israeli border. The Multinational Force and Observers (MFO) was established in 1982, upon the expiration of the UN mandate. This is an independent international organization, financed equally by the Arab Republic of Egypt, Israel, and the United States of America, with special contributions from the governments of Germany and of Japan. This organization has been given the task of observing and verifying that the peace treaty is observed; among its duties is that of reporting on any violations of the limitations on military personnel and infrastructure in the four zones covered, as well as that of ensuring free passage through the Strait of Tiran and in the waters of the southern Gulf of Eilat. The four zones are called, respectively, Zone A, Zone B, Zone C and Zone D. In Zone A, Egypt may maintain an infantry division of twenty-two thousand men, with their military installations and field fortifications, such as early alarm systems.
In Zone B, Egypt can maintain four battalions of four thousand men, along with their military installations, field fortifications, and coastal observation points with short-range armaments.
In Zone C, only members of the MFO are allowed, though Egypt is allowed to maintain civilian police units, armed with light rifles.
In Zone D, in Israel, there are four Israeli infantry battalions with a

total of four thousand men, as an early alert force. The MFO still performs a perfectly legitimate function, and anyone who visits the Sinai will soon notice the constant coming and going of vehicles with plates reading MFO, and emblazoned with the dove of peace, as drawn by Pablo Picasso. The nations that form part of the MFO are Australia, Canada, Colombia, the Fiji Islands, France, Italy, the Netherlands, New Zealand, the United States of America, and Uruguay. These military units are distributed in two base camps: the north camp at Gorah (twenty kilometers, or about twelve miles, to the south of the Mediterranean coast), and the south camp at Sharm el-Sheikh. Italy is present with three minesweeping gunboats anchored in the military port of Sharm el-Sheikh; Italy's mission here is to ensure freedom of navigation in the Strait of Tiran and in the southern mouth of the Gulf of Eilat.

12 top The great bay of Naama opens out immediately north of Sharm el-Sheikh, and in just a few years, its tourist facilities have completely occupied the coast, transforming this bay into the most important tourist attraction in the Sinai.

12 center By the sea, at the mouth of a vast wadi, is the little town of Dahab, a name that in the Beduin tongue, means "gold," with clear reference to the sands of the beaches.

12 bottom One of the jobs of the men of the MFO is to supervise the transit of the trucks that travel through the Zone C, ensuring that there is no movement of unauthorized military vehicles. In this picture, we see a checkpoint of the MFO along the road that leads to Saint Catherine.

13 bottom In accordance with international agreements, the Egyptian Sinai was split up into three zones (A, B, and C) while to the east, in Israeli territory, there is a fourth zone, called D. In these areas, the presence of military forces is regulated in the strictest possible manner, and the checkpoints are manned by an international force known as the M.F.O., or "Multinational Force and Observers."

13 top Italy is one of the nations that has a military contingent which forms part of the MFO; three minesweepers of the Italian navy are stationed in the bay of Sharm el-Sheikh.

13 center The Italian minesweeper Mango is shown steaming through the strait of Tiran.

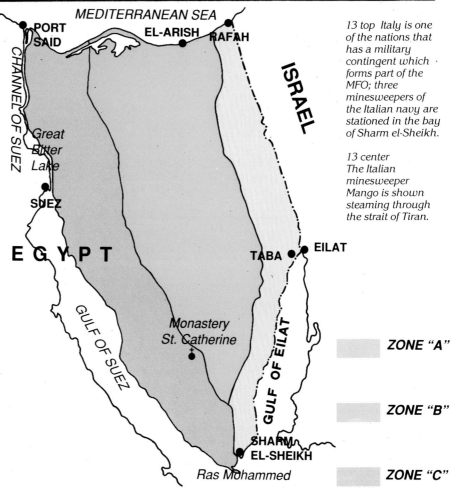

ZONE "A"

ZONE "B"

ZONE "C"

THE BEDUINS OF THE SINAI

The Beduins are, by definition, a nomadic desert people; this is indicated quite clearly by their name, which derives from the Arabic word *bedu*, meaning "inhabitant of the desert": the great expanses of sand and the harsh desert mountains are their chosen habitat, where they hold unquestioned sway.

These are people accustomed to living one's whole lifetime in a tent, with the their camels and goats, moving in accordance with the seasons and the requirements of their grazing livestock.

Dressed in their long *djellabas*, or full, loose-fitting garments of wool or cotton, with hood and sleeves and skirt; in long white tunics, and *kaffiyehs*, or headdresses consisting of a square of cloth folded to form a triangle and bound with an *agal*, or double-braided cord, originally made of goat hair, today usually made of cotton fiber.

Dressed as they are, we imagine them to be men of the desert, surveying their arid kingdom from atop a camel.

This is a society based on tribal bonds, subject nowadays to profound and radical changes, destined to undergo a long slow metamorphosis that is likely to coincide with a progressive loss of identity.

The Beduins, split into some fifty tribes, occupy an exceedingly extensive area, covering the Arabian peninsula, Syria, Jordan, Israel, the Sinai, and the eastern desert: in the Sinai, the fifty thousand or so Beduins are split up into roughly ten tribes, the product of mergers of other, older tribes with later arrivals to the peninsula, some of whom have only arrived recently.

14 top A young unmarried Beduin woman shows herself with an uncovered face, but her head covered with a veil that covers the hair arranged in braids.

14 bottom The camel once represented a very important feature in the life of the desert nomads. Replaced nowadays in travel and everyday use by the automobile,

the camel has become mainly a tourist attraction, even though it does remain the only useful means of exploration in the most inaccessible areas of the Sinai.

15 top
The distinctive headgear worn by Beduin men is constituted of a strip of cloth called a kaffiyeh, held by a doubled cord called an agal.

15 center
A Beduin woman has her face covered by the distinctive burka, to which are attached bangles and coins of gold and brass.

15 bottom A small Beduin girl, her head covered in the traditional manner, smiles at the photographer.

15 bottom right This drawing shows the distribution of the various Beduin tribes of the Sinai.

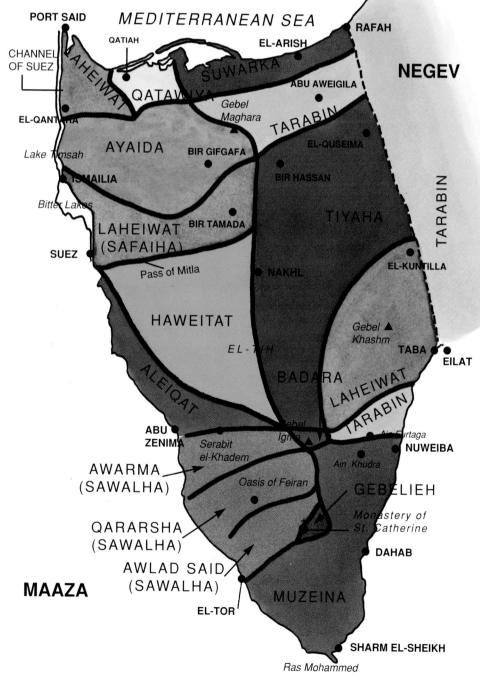

THE BEDUINS OF THE NORTHERN SINAI

As far as the Beduins living in the north and central Sinai, these consist of a few large tribes that have incorporated a number of lesser tribes and clans: the Suwarka, the most numerous, live in the territories along the Mediterranean coast of the Sinai, starting around the area of Bir el-Abd, while further south there are two other, smaller tribes: the Qatawiya near Bir Qatia, and the Masaid, who occupy the territory that runs from the village of Rumani to the Suez Canal. The Tarabin, Palestinian in origin, have settled in the region of Gebel Maghara, Gebel Hallal, and Abu Aweigila. Further south, on the other hand, live the Tiyaha, also of Palestinian origin, who occupy an enormous territory which includes the oasis of el-Quseima in the north, the small town of Nakhl to the west, and as far as the oasis of el-Kuntilla to the south. Affilitated with the Tiyaha are the representatives of the small tribe of the Badara, who live in the region of Gebel Igma. In the area to the south of the territory occupied by the Tiyaha, between el-Kuntilla and Aqaba, live the Lahelwat, a sub-tribe of whom — known as the Safalha — have settled in the northernmost section of the coast of the Gulf of Suez and along the channel that runs to the Bitter Lakes, and eastward as far as Gifgafa and Tamad. Between the territory of the Lahelwat and that of the Tiyaha lives the great tribe of the Haweitat, of Jordanian origins, who occupy a triangular area to the southeast of Suez, around the area of Gebel Raha. Lastly, the tribe of the Alayda occupies the territory between the Suez Canal, to the north of Ismailia and the Gebel Maghara.

16 top The clothing of Beduin women indicates their social status: in this photograph, one can see a married woman with her face partially covered by a hood known as the "waqa," which is in turn covered by a strip of material to which bangles and coins of silver and gold are attached to make the classic "burqa."

16 center Two Beduins, their camels saddled and ready to carry tourists, north of Naama Bay. For these tribesmen, already in large part settled and no longer nomadic, tourism has become a profitable way of life.

16 bottom The classic Beduin tent, the very symbol of the nomadic way of life, is becoming increasingly rare, replaced by shacks made of sheet metal, cardboard, or bits of wood.

THE TRIBES OF THE SOUTHERN SINAI OR THE TOWARAS

The first two tribes to settle in the Sinai, at the time of the Muslim conquest of Egypt, the Aleiqat and the Sawalha, were later joined by the Muzeina and thereafter by the Maaza, today largely located in the Eastern Desert along the shores of the Red Sea, and on the mountains that run parallel to that shore, slightly to the west, and the Howeitat. All of these tribes, or varied origins but all settlers in the Sinai peninsula and in turn split up into an array of sub-groups, are indicated collectively with the name of Towaras, or Arabs of el-Tor. The Aleiqat are located in the area around Abu Zenima and along the shores of the Gulf of Suez; it is reasonable to link the Aleiqat with the Tarabin, who have settled both to the north of Nuweiba and in the northern Sinai (in the region of el-Arish and in the area around the Gebel Maghara), although many of them live in Jordan and Israel.

The Sawalha include three other tribes: the Awarma, the Qararsha, and the Awlad Said, and live on the outskirts of el-Tor.

The Muzeina, on the other hand, make their base along the shores of the Gulf of Eilat.

To these groups, we should add the Hitheim, who do not constitute a full-fledged tribe, but rather a heterogeneous group with all sorts of origins, often the result of the breakdown of small local tribes. The Hitheim, who have settled in the Sinai as well as in the Hedjaz region in Jordan, are great breeders of camels, but are otherwise held in low esteem by the other Beduins. Lastly, the Djebelieh, a name that means "mountaineers," are a case that stands alone, since these are not true Beduins, but simply descendents of the group of families, originally from Bosnia and Walachia who were assigned by the emperor Justinian to serve in the Monastery of Saint Catherine. In some cases, certain of these mountain people clearly display facial features that might surprise one, such as blue eyes or

17 top Large saddlebags, perfectly suited to containing foodstuffs and other objects complete the fittings of the camel. The colors and motifs of the decoration vary, according to region and tribe.

17 center
The grinding stone used by the Beduins in the production of the flour needed to bake their unleavened bread. This grinding stone is called "aesh," and is very similar to the grinding stones used by the peoples of the Neolithic, when they abandoned the hunting and gathering economy in order to devote themselves to the more sedentary economy of farming and livestock breeding.

17 bottom
The Beduin camel saddle is made up of a wooden framework made up of a fairly simple structure that includes two upside-down V's, connected on each side by two X-shaped joints. This framework is then covered with fabric and hides to make it more comfortable.

18 top The Beduins of the tribe of the Gebeliah, who live in the region surrounding the monastery of St. Catherine, live on their earnings as guides and as trekking scouts. The splendid hiking paths that wend through these mountains can only be travelled by humans on foot, or, along certain stretches, on camelback. More than for the transport of human beings, however, camels are usually used here to carry food and water, needed by those who live in the mountains for a number of days.

18 bottom Selim Barakat Selim, of the Beduin family of the Barakat, exercises authority over the region of Serabit el-Khadem: in this area which has still not been hit heavily by tourism, the ritual involved in the preparation of shai, the Beduin tea, remains an important moment during the day's activities.

red hair, and this is a result of their European origin.

The Gebeliah — who soon converted to Islam, although they continued to perform their functions in the monastery — are in fact called the *Sebayat el-Deir*, which means, "the Servants of the Convent," and much like the Hitheim, which whom they are somehow associated, they are held in universally low esteem. Today, this overall scheme or description is subject to incessant variations and changes, because the process through which the Beduins are becoming a sedentary people, which began during the nineteenth century, has accelerated over recent years: the tents are being replaced by fairly temporary shelters and lean-tos made of sheet metal; from the roof protrudes the inevitable television antenna; camels are being replaced by small Toyota pickup trucks; grazing is being replaced by tourism. There are ever increasing number of Beduins being integrated into the tourist industry, both as guides and as drivers, or else in organized camel tours through the desert, crowned by the inevitable "Beduin feast," which basically consists of an old tradition of theirs evoked for the enjoyment of the tourists.

The traditions, customs, and garb of the Beduin have changed radically from what they used to be. Their legendary hospitality, accompanied by the unfailing offering of *shai bil nana*, the classic mint tea, is nowadays nothing more than a service provided in exchange for payment; it has become the rule that when a tourist photographs not only a Beduin, but even a tent or just a camel, he or she must pay a certain fee, according to rates that are unwritten but are quite specific and well known. One can hardly blame the Beduins for their behavior: after all, these former nomads, now becoming a sedentary people, have been forced to adapt radically in order to survive in a world that becomes harsher and more hostile with every day that passes. The few tourists, however, who have the courage and the desire to leave the beaten track and to venture out into the wildest wastes of the mountains of the Sinai, on foot or by camel, will certainly discover, sooner or later, some small group of Beduins who have chosen the path of non-integration, and so if the traveller then acts with discretion and intelligence, he or she will discover what remains of an ancient culture, founded upon great and enduring ideals: honor, pride, courage, and hospitality.

19 top In this photograph, taken along the coast to the south of Nuweiba, two young Beduin girls are shown, dressed in their traditional outfits.

19 center Fishing for small crustaceans, which is done largely off the coast and by women, is an important activity for the Beduins of Dahab.

19 bottom Around the well of the oasis of Ain Hudra, there have been settlements of Beduin tribes since the earliest times, as is shown also by the great number of rock carvings in the area.

This important watering spot lies along the route of the caravan routes which run along the Wadi Hudra and the Wadi Ghazala, linking the region of Nuweiba with the region of Saint Catherine.

THE ISTHMUS AND THE CANAL OF SUEZ

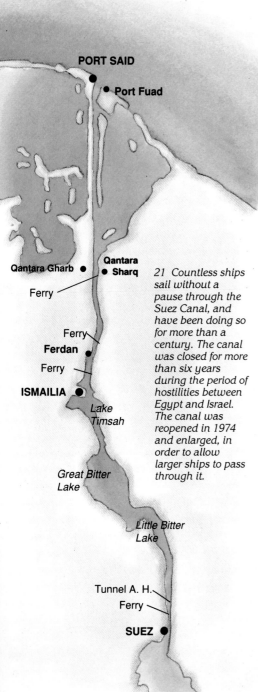

20 On the horizon, one can see the skyline of the modern buildings of the port area of

Suez, known as Port Tawfik. Suez was largely destroyed during the Six-Day War.

The isthmus of Suez is a sandy strip of land that extends some one hundred sixty-four kilometers (almost precisely a hundred miles) along a north-south axis, interrupted by three closed bodies of water: Lake Timsah, to the north; and the Bitter Lakes to the south. This strip of land separates the Red Sea from the Mediterranean, and the Nile Delta from the Sinai peninsula.
This natural barrier, which lies betwixt the two great seas of the ancient world, represented a considerable obstacle to the development of commerce. Ever since ancient times, men dreamed of changing their natural environment and of digging a canal which might facilitate communications along the north-south route between the Red Sea and the Mediterranean. The first time that a waterway was laid down through the isthmus of Suez, however, it did not actually lead from the Mediterranean to

until a century had passed, around 510 B.C., by Darius, king of Persia: the canal ran from the Nile to a point in line with the city of Bubastis, then if followed the Wadi Tumilath and entered Lake Timsah, whence it extended to the Gulf of Suez. This waterway remained in operation until the time of Alexander; it was later reopened and utilized by the Roman emperors, especially by Trajan. During the time of Arab domination, around A.D. 645, the ancient canal was restored, and used to carry trade between the Nile Valley and Mecca; around the end of the eighth century A.D., however, because of economic difficulties, the canal was abandoned, and was gradually filled up with sand. Later, even the Republic of Venice — which possessed the most important merchant fleet in the Mediterranean, and which practically held a monopoly on eastern trade — studied the

21 Countless ships sail without a pause through the Suez Canal, and have been doing so for more than a century. The canal was closed for more than six years during the period of hostilities between Egypt and Israel. The canal was reopened in 1974 and enlarged, in order to allow larger ships to pass through it.

the Red Sea; rather it joined the Red Sea with the Nile, through Lake Timsah. This event probably dates from the Middle Kingdom, from the reign of Sesostris I, around 2,000 B.C.. Even though no traces remain of this canal, Herodotus nonetheless tells us that, around 600 B.C., the pharaoh Necao decided to undertake the enormous task of building a canal on the Suez Isthmus (see Historiae, II, 158). The project, however, was abandoned upon the death of the sovereign, and was not resumed

possibility of digging a waterway that would cross the isthmus of Suez, but the lagoon city gave up on the idea; the Venetian State Archives, in fact, preserve a parchment dated 1504, in which the project of excavating the canal was presented to the Council of Ten. It was necessary to wait until the nineteenth century, and more precisely, until 25 April 1859, when work began once again on the digging of a great canal, this time at the insistence of the French diplomat, Ferdinand De Lesseps, whose project received ample support from prince Said, the future khedive of Egypt. Ten years of hard work were required before the mammoth task could be completed, but on 17 November 1869 the Suez Canal was officially opened, when the khedive and the empress Eugénie, the wife of Napoleon III, made the sail from Port Said to Suez, aboard the imperial yacht. For the first time in human history, a direct water link had been established between the Red Sea and the Mediterranean. Since the immense amount of money that had been required to complete the project had been obtained through investments of foreign capital, in the form of the "Compagnie du Canal de Suez," this company obtained a concession for the exclusive operation of the canal for ninety-nine years. The military importance of this canal, as well as its importance to trade, may have been underestimated at the outset, but it grew greatly over the years following its inauguration, and in 1875, the British Crown decided to purchase 44 percent of the shares in the company.

Later, in 1888, the leading nations of Europe agreed to the Treaty of Constantinople, which ensured freedom of navigation through the canal, and its neutrality.

At the beginning of the 1950s, with the succession of Nasser to power in Egypt, with his socialist and nationalist political programs, the independence of the Suez Canal began to be perceived as a threat to the sovereignty of Egypt, and on 26 July 1956, the Suez Canal was nationalized and removed from the control of the Company, which theoretically held a lease on it that would not expire until 1968. A few months later, on 5 November, the leading European powers, France and Great Britain, responded to Nasser's expropriation by stationing troops along the canal zone, at Port Said, at Port Fuad, and at Ismailia, but the intervention of the United States and the U.S.S.R. in the United Nations blocked this action, and the French and British troops were

obliged to retire at the end of December in the same year, and Egypt won recognition of its inviolable sovereignty over the Suez Canal. Although Nasser had agreed to respect the Treaty of Constantinople, Israeli ships had no right of passage through the canal, and this uneven situation generated a state of increasingly high tension, which ended with the blockage of the Strait of Tiran by the Arab nations, with the consequential Israeli response, which resulted in the Six-Day War. During that war, Israel seized the Sinai, and reached the shores of the Suez Canal which, for the first time in its history, remained closed for more than six years, until the beginning of 1974. Then new dredging work was undertaken, so as to deepen and widen the canal, and Israeli ships obtained the right of passage in compliance with the Treaty of Constantinople. Today, anyone who travels to the Sinai by land is, obviously, forced to go cross the canal; in order to facilitate this passage, which had once been obliged to rely upon the many ferryboats moored to the north of

Suez, to the north of Ismailia, and at Ferdan and el-Qantara, a tunnel sixteen hundred meters (almost exactly a mile) in length was inaugurated.

This tunnel runs beneath the canal, making it easier, faster, and more reliable to cross the canal, although the ferryboats still run. The tunnel, whose construction required five years of work, was dedicated to an officer of the Egyptian army who was killed in 1973, during the October War: Ahmed Hamdi.

NORTHERN SINAI

The northernmost section of the Sinai peninsula, the coastline of which is bathed by the waters of the Mediterranean Sea, is a territory rich in natural beauty as well as major archeological remains. This vast area - because of the relative absence of infrastructure for tourists, but especially because of the almost total lack of information concerning this area in guidebooks and other publications about the Sinai peninsula - is almost totally ignored by the majority of tourists travelling alone, and almost entirely left out of the programs of major tour operators. All the same, all those who decide to "explore" the northern Sinai will be pleasantly astonished at the beauty of the landscapes and the wealth of archeological finds, artifacts, and monuments dotting an area that,

until the decline of the pharaohs, was of enormous strategic importance, inasmuch as it represented the main route between Egypt and the east (through here ran the so-called Track of Horus, which the pharaohs would travel, with their armies, when conducting military campaigns in the east). It later witnessed the development of a number of major urban centers, which developed in particular around the Persian era and during Greek and Roman times. Unfortunately, due to the inevitable need to reclaim new areas to make room for the burgeoning population of Egypt, with the resulting construction of new roads, new channels and watercourses, and new urban centers, in accordance with a plan approved by the Egyptian Government in 1990, many of the archeological areas of the northern Sinai will be destroyed.

The Egyptian Antiquities Organization is undertaking a plan for the rescue and salvage of the endangered areas through the creation of a great many archeological digging campaigns, led by Egyptian and non-Egyptian archeologists. This work is producing a great deal of valuable information, considerably enriching our historical knowledge concerning this area.

ITINERARIES

FROM THE SUEZ CANAL TO EL-ARISH (coastal route)

The paved road, that runs parallel with the Mediterranean coast of the Sinai, also connects the Suez Canal with the city of el-Arish, the capital of the northern Sinai, and continues as far as Rafah, where the Israeli border is located; the road begins at the city of el-Qantara Sharq (meaning "Eastern el-Qantara"), which can be reached either by taking the road that starts at Tunnel A.H. and then cuts north, running alongside the Suez Canal, or else by taking the ferryboat that crosses the Suez Canal to the north of Ismailia el-Qantara at Gharb (meaning "Western el-Qantara"). After passing through the new urban center called New Qantara Sharq, still under construction and located near the archeological site of Tell Abu Seifa, one reaches a checkpoint, and then one continues on to the site of Tell el-Herr, near the village of Galbana. This site extends over an area of about thirty hectares (seventy-five acres), and many scholars identify it as the site of the "fortress of Midgol," which is mentioned in the Bible. After travelling sixteen kilometers (ten miles) past the checkpoint, and just prior to entering the little village of Balouza (which takes its name directly from Pelusium, about which more below), one finds, on the left, a paved road, marked by a large sign that points one toward the site of Tell el-Farama, which corresponds to the ancient city of Pelusium, the most important archeological site in all of the northern Sinai, where the Egyptian Antiquities Organization is conducting a vast and far-reaching

22 The ruins of the city of Pelusium stretch over a vast area of the easternmost section of the Nile Delta, and today major archeological excavations are underway there. Pelusium, which surveyed the routes that linked Egypt with the East, was particularly powerful between the seventh century B.C. and the sixth century A.D.

digging campaign. After travelling a few kilometers, or miles, toward the north, one reaches the archeological area, on either side of the road.

PELUSIUM, THE "GATE OF EGYPT"

What is now called Tell el-Farama was once a fortified city that in the time of the pharaohs was called *Peremun*, meaning "that which Amun has created." This ancient survives in the modern name of Farama, although the site is better known by its Greek name of *Pelousion*, meaning "marsh." This name reappears in the place-name of the nearby village of Balouza. The city of Pelusium, near which lies the easternmost branch of the Nile Delta - the so-called "Pelusiac branch" - was considered as early as the seventh century B.C. to be the "gateway into Egypt," inasmuch as it commanded access to the Delta from the east. The city became an increasingly important center during the Persian era and, subsequently, during the Thirtieth Dynasty and during the Ptolemaic Period. Toward the first and second centuries B.C., Hebrews and Romans took up residence in Pelusium, and the Holy Family during the Flight into Egypt stopped in Pelusium. After a period of obscurity, Pelusium regained its importance between the first and third centuries A.D., becoming a major cultural center when, following a visit from the emperor Hadrian (A.D. 138), the city was declared an "Eastern Roman City." Later on, Diocletian, too, came to Pelusium. In the fourth century, during the reign of Constantine, the city became a bishopric and the capital of a new province, which included the northern Sinai and the eastern Delta, a necessary part of the route followed by the pilgrims who were travelling from the Holy Land to the Sinai. This religious fervor is documented by the numerous religious buildings that have been uncovered by archeological excavations. One example is the large church with three naves excavated at Tell el-Makhzan,

situated at the easternmost extremity of Pelusium. In the sixth century, during the reign of Justinian, Pelusium was still a major port; in time, the sand choked the "Pelusiac branch," resulting in an ineluctable decline of the city and its fall into oblivion. Returning to the main road that leads to el-Arish, one travels for another thirteen kilometers (eight miles), and then one arrives in the village of Rumana: from this point forward, there is a paved road that leads to the Mediterranean coast, which for a long stretch is separated from the open sea by a narrow littoral barrier strip that forms a huge lagoon, extending over a surface area of sixty thousand hectares (148,200 acres), known as Lake Bardawil. This is a protected area of great interest to a naturalist, because this is the stopover area for countless migrating birds, as well as being a major nesting area. The classical authors called it *Lacus Sirbonis*, but Lake Bardawil owes its modern name to the imperfect transliteration of the name "Baldwin" into Arabic. Apparently, during the First Crusade, which was led by Baldwin, the first Latin king of Jersualem, a fortified outpost was built near the lagoon, which was given the name of the future king. The area around Lake Bardawil also has great historical interest inasmuch as it lay along the main track that connected Egypt with the east; according to those who

support the so-called "northern route" for the Exodus, Lake Bardawil corresponds to the site where the Hebrews made their famous "passage through the Red Sea," pursued by the pharaoh's army. The Bible (see Exodus, 14), in fact, calls the site of the crossing *yam suf*, which is correctly translated as the "sea of reeds," and not at all Red Sea, as it has traditionally been interpreted. This definition of a "sea of reeds" can be applied to two different areas, that of the Bitter Lakes and Lake Timsah, the basins that are now crossed by the Suez Canal, and that of Lake Bardawil. The former identification is supported by the classical interpretation of the itinerary of the Exodus, while the supporters of the so-called "northern route" indicate Lake Bardawil, maintaining, and with some reason, that in the case of the Bitter Lakes the pharaoh's armies could easily have worked their way around the obstacles, lying in wait for the fugitives on the other side of the swampy area of the Bitter Lakes. The strategic importance of Lake Bardawil is documented by the presence not only of fortified cities which controlled access from the west, but also by settlements built close to the lagoon. The littoral strip which is responsible for the formation of Lake Bardawil is made up of a narrow sandy spit, dominated to the east by a tall sand dune called el-Guels, which has been identified with the *Mons*

23 Sand dunes, dotted with extensive grassy scrub, among which the camels browse, constitute the typical landscape of the northern Sinai coast.

Kasios mentioned by classical authors (in honor of Juppiter Kasios), corresponding to the ancient coast line, before the waters of the Mediterranean invaded the lower-lying stretches of the coast, following the general rise in the planet's sea levels; this last-named shift, known as the "Flandrian transgression," took place during the Quaternarian Period, some eight thousand years ago. Along this sandy belt, recent explorations have allowed scientists to determine the site of the ancient port of *Gerrah*, near the promontory now known as Mohammedia, as well as fortress dating from the First Intermediate Period, which was rebuilt during

the reign of Sethos I, identified as the anceint *Tcharu*, and located on the site called Tell Hebua.

If we continue along the main road that winds through the desert landscape, amidst golden sand dunes dotted with dense shrubs and patches of grass, and occasionally with groups of tall majestic palms, one will often encounter groups of Bedouins, generally tribesmen of the Suwarka; they live in huts and tents near the many springs that are found not far from the road. After driving thirty-four kilometers (twenty-one miles) from Rumana', one reaches the small Bedouin village of Bir el-Abd, meaning "the well of the slave." Here a

track, heading south, begins allowing one to reach the archeological site of Kasserwit, where excavations have unearthed remains from Roman times and a number of fragments from temples and Nabataean tombs. After passing by Bir el-Abd, and travelling another fifty kilometers (about thirty miles) or so, one will see on the left a road that leads to the wildlife area of Zaranik, sitauted on the eastern extremity of Lake Bardawil. The road also leads to the small fishing port of Flusya (a place-name that derives from the Arabic word *filus*, meaning "money"; the name appears to come from the fact that the Bedouins would often dig up coins dating from Roman times here), near which are the ruins of the Roman settlement of *Ostrakine*, and of two Byzantine churches. The area around Zaranik, populated by vast numbers of migratory birds, is particularly interesting in terms of ornithological observations, especially during the months of September-October and March-April. Although access to Lake Bardawil is strictly limited in order to maintain the lake's environmental qualities and in order to protect its wildlife, it is possible to ask for a visitor's permit by applying to the North Sinai Governatorate Environmental Office at el-Arish. If one continues along the main road that runs

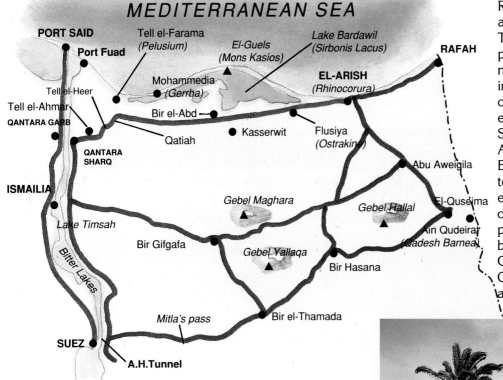

MEDITERRANEAN SEA

PORT SAID
Port Fuad
Tell el-Farama
(Pelusium)
El-Guels
(Mons Kasios)
Lake Bardawil
(Sirbonis Lacus)
RAFAH
Tell el-Heer
Mohammedia
(Gerrha)
EL-ARISH
(Rhinocorura)
Tell el-Ahmar
QANTARA GARB
Bir el-Abd
QANTARA SHARQ
Qatiah
Kasserwit
Flusiya
(Ostrakine)
Abu Aweiqila
ISMAILIA
Gebel Maghara
Gebel Hallal
El-Quseima
Lake Timsah
Ain Qudeirat
(Qadesh Barnea)
Bitter Lakes
Bir Gifgafa
Gebel Yallaqa
Bir Hasana
Mitla's pass
Bir el-Thamada
SUEZ
A.H.Tunnel

24 The celebrated palm grove that once constituted one of the major attractions of the beach of el-Arish, in ancient times a city named Rhinocorura, and today administrative capital of the northern Sinai, has mostly been destroyed in order to make room for new houses and tourist facilities.

25 Two Beduins, their heads covered with the kaffiyeh, *as in bygone times, ride their camels along the desert tracks.*

increasingly close to the Mediterranean coast, flanked in numerous points by tall palm trees, one will arrive at the checkpoint guarding the outskirts of el-Arish. This checkpoint is located at a distance of twenty-three kilometers (fourteen miles) past the fork in the road for Zaranik, and one hundred and forty kilometers (eighty-eight miles) past the checkpoint of el-Qantara, and right across from a service station with a gas pump, where the road to the airport starts. Continuing along toward the city, one must drive another ten kilometers (six miles) to get to the center, where the main hotels are located, the only hotels in the entire region. El-Arish, the capital of the Governatorate of the North Sinai, has a population of about seventy thousand; not only is it the most important city in the region, but it also has the most popular beach and bathing areas. It owes its reputation to its broad beach, long ago bounded by a wonderful grove of palm trees which, sadly, is nowadays only a memory, as the tall palm trees have made way for cement and the motley constructions built directly on the sand. The easternmost outpost of the empire of the pharaohs, el-Arish was the site of the Ptolemaic and Roman fortress of *Rhinocorura*, a border stronghold which was also the destination for many exiles. On the ruins of this settlement, during the Middle Ages, a fortified city was built; by 1482, however, when the traveller Joos van Ghistele visited here, the city no longer existed. Later, in 1560, a new fortress was built in the area by the sultan Suleiman el-Khanuni; this fortress was destroyed by bombardment during the First World War. The scanty fragments of this fort can be seen in the neighborhood known as Fuakhariya, where there is an interesting Bedouin market every Wednesday. Even if el-Arish nowadays possesses no remarkable attractions in terms of landscape or wildlife, it is an interesting place to visit because of the quality and variety of the Bedouin handicrafts, and because of the excellent ethnographic museum, devoted to the culture of the Sinai Bedouin. This is the Sinai Heritage Museum, located in the eastern section of the city, not far from the headquarters of the Governatorate, along the road that leads to the border outpost of

Rafah. After passing the museum and the intersection with the road that leads, first to the airport, and subsequently to el-Quseima, Nakhl, or Ismailia (see itinerary el-Arish-Suez), one takes this road and travels a distance of thirty kilometers (almost twenty miles), and then one will reach the village Sheikh Zuweid, on a line with which is an archeological site dating from Roman times. This site has not yet been excavated systematically, but archeologists did unearth a splendid mosaic depicting Sheikh Zuweid, dating from the fourth century A.D., now in the collection of the museum of Ismailia. From Sheikh Zuweid, it is possible to reach a handsome beach, dominated by a pillar of red granite, brought here from Gebel Musa by the Israeli to commemorate a helicopter that crashed here in 1971. One can also continue eastward another fourteen kilometers (nine miles), and reach Rafah, a small village at the easternmost tip of the Egyptian coastline. To the north of the modern-day village, archeologists have found (but have not yet excavated) the ancient Ptolemaic and Roman site of *Rafia*. Here, in 217 B.C., a battle was fought that resulted in the destruction of the army of Antioch III of Syria by the troops led by Ptolemy IV Philopator. Rafah also lies on border with Israel, which runs down from here as far as Taba in the Gulf of Aqaba, marking the ancient boundary line between the Sinai and the Ottoman Empire, a boundary that was drawn at the behest of the British back in 1906. Nowadays there is a newly built road that allows a direct link between Rafah and Taba.

FROM EL-ARISH TO THE SUEZ CANAL (inland road)

In line with the easternmost point of el-Arish, where the museum and the Governatorate are located, a road starts out which runs southeast, leading first to the airport that lies some ten kilometers (six miles) outside of the city. Another ten kilometers (six miles) further on there is a fork in the road. From here, taking the road on the left, which runs southeast, one reaches

the villages of Abu Aweigla and el-Quseima from where, taking the track that runs eastward, one can reach the major archeological site of Ain Qudeirat, identified as the Biblical site of Qadesh-Barnea, from which Moses sent out emissaries to explore the land of Canaan. Over a fairly extensive area, the excavations have brought to light the structures corresponding to three fortresses which were built successively between the tenth and the sixth centuries B.C. If one takes the road leading to the right, on the other hand, after thirty-eight

kilometers (twenty-four miles), one will run into an intersection with the road that runs here directly from the village of Abu Aweigla, and, another four kilometers (two-and-a-half miles) further on, there is a fork in the road where one can turn south and then reach, first, Bir Hasana and then the city of Nakhl, near which the road, after joining back up with the road from Tunnel A.H., heads off toward Taba-Nuweiba. If one continues westward, on the other hand, skirting the southern edge of the massif of Gebel Maghara (do not confuse this one with the mountain of the same name in the south-central Sinai). It is made up of limestone formations from the Jurassic Era. The road leads on to the oasis of Bir Gifgafa, whence another road sets off which once led to the coast, near Bir el-Abd - it is now covered in part by tall sand dunes. From Bir Gifgafa, the road continues westward, through the Pass of Khatmia, and - after a distance of fifty-five kilometers (thirty-four miles) - it intersects the road that skirts the Suez Canal.

THE WEST COAST OF THE SINAI

TUNNEL AHMED HAMDI - EL-TOR - SHARM EL-SHEIKH

The west coast of the Sinai looks out over the waters of the Gulf of Suez: the northernmost section is low-lying and sandy, while the south central section is bounded by mountainous outcroppings of the Sinai massif, which here take the form of limestone formations. The Gulf of Suez has a geological history that is quite different from that of the Gulf of Eilat; the absence of major tectonic phenomena explains its shallowness. The Gulf of Suez, where a great many ships enter and leave the Suez Canal, is extremely polluted; the presence of tar on the beaches and the almost complete absence of coral formations make the western coast of the Sinai peninsula far less interesting and beautiful than the eastern coast, even if there is no shortage of reasonably interesting spots along this route, which takes one rapidly to Saint Catherine, via Wadi Feiran, and to Ras Mohammed and Sharm el-Sheikh.

Itinerary

After passing through the Tunnel Ahmed Hamdi, first one reaches the major intersection that marks the beginning of the road leading to Nuweiba, via Nakhl. First there is a gas station (kilometer 5.5 - or mile 3.5 - from the tunnel) and then a fork in the road (kilometer 16.5 - or mile 10 - from the tunnel); at this fork, keep to the left, following the signs for el-Tor. The road runs along a monotonous and desolate plain, upon which one can see numerous signs of the war with Israel: the wreckage of tanks, the remains of artillery emplacements, bits of military trucks, bunkers, and the ruins of military fortifications. These pieces of military history constitute a genuine "open-air museum," especially in the area surrounding the little coffee shop that stands just before Ayun Musa. At kilometer 22.5 - or mile 14 - from the tunnel, and two kilometers, or just over a mile, before a checkpoint manned by the Egyptian army, on one's right is the site of Ayun Musa, meaning the "Wells of Moses," where, according to tradition, Moses made camp following the crossing of the Red Sea and, miraculously, brought forth water from the sands. Ayun Musa was also one of the stops along the land route followed by the Muslim pilgrims who were returning from their pilgrimage to Mecca. In the midst of a dense stand of palm trees and tamarisks (at a distance from the road of about two hundred fifty meters, or some eight hundred feet), it is possible to see a number of circular wells, at the bottom of which bubbles a spring of brackish water. Only one spring, situated about a kilometer, or three-quarters of a mile, to the southwest of the stand of palm trees, and somewhat downhill, offers an abundance of fresh water, at a temperature that indicates its thermal origins. This spring has been harnessed to serve man, however, and its waters run through a large pipe and are put to the use of the local Beduins. Ayun Musa enjoys a flourishing bird population and is also a stopover point in the migratory routes of a great number of birds of prey. After travelling on past Ayun Musa, the road begins to wind though a monotonous landscape inevitably spangled with wind-blasted trophies of war: over this stretch of road it is particularly dangerous to leave the road, because landmines and entire mine fields are common in the land on either side of the road. And so one reaches Ras Sudr (sixty-one kilometers, or about forty miles from the Tunnel) where large metal tanks indicate the presence of a large petroleum refinery. A gas station, a tire repair shop, and a coffee shop can be found at the intersection with the road that leads to the little town of Ras Sudr; off to the west, toward the beach, is the Sudr Beach Hotel. Four kilometers, or about two-and-a-half miles past Ras Sudr, at Abu Suweira, one can see on the left the road that leads to the imposing fortress of Qalaat el-Qundi, which means "the Fortress of the Soldier," built by the sultan Salah el-Din, better known as Saladin (see itinerary). Now the road beings to run through the vast Wadi Wardan, and the landscape is dominated by a series of sand dunes. Then one reaches Ras Materma (81.5 kilometers, or about fifty miles from the Tunnel) where a broad beach stretches out with a camp grounds and the tourist village of Dagashland. After passing a long beach (100.5 kilometers, or about sixty-one miles from the Tunnel) and the promontory of Ras Malaab, the road winds between the coast and the mountain; here the mountain begins to display the chalky rocks that are so typical of this region and close of the other of Wadi Gharandal. On the right, at a distance of one hundred ten kilometers, or about seventy miles

27 top The famed springs of Ayun Musa, the "fountains of Moses" where, according to tradition, Moses halted his people on the flight out of Egypt, and made the brackish water drinkable.

27 center The wreckage of tanks and armored trucks, abundant in the area around Ayun Musa, offer mute testimony to the harsh fighting between Egyptians and Israelis, constituting a sort of "open-air" museum.

27 bottom The mountains that border the west coast of the Sinai are largely made up of rocks of undersea origins, such as limestone and sandstone.

from the Tunnel), one can see a small road that leads to the sit of Hammam Faraun Malun, "the Baths of the Cursed Pharaoh," where, according to legend, the cursed pharaoh would be the one that chased with his war chariots after the Hebrews who were fleeing across the Red Sea after it miraculously parted; the pharaoh of course was destroyed when the waters closed after the Hebrews, and was lost with all his army. In this site of great beauty, dominated by a pyramid-shaped limestone mountain hot sulphureous

waters gush forth (this is a form of contact thermalism), pouring directly into the sea. (Hammam Faraun closes at 6 pm. In order to reach the beach it is necessary to leave the documents for one's vehicle at a military checkpoint). Seven kilometers, or about four-and-a-half miles past the little road that leads to Hammam Faraun, one passes the little detour that leads to the tiny oasis of Wadi Gharandal, and one reaches the area around Wadi Tayiba (134 kilometers, or about eighty-four miles from the Tunnel); the distinctive features of the location are a stand of palm trees and a track that allows one to climb up the wadi and admire pristine nature and a landscape shaped by the waters that have modelled the limestone and the miocene marls, which here emerge in striking upthrusts. The oasis of Tayiba, which had been a major trading spot and caravan stopover until the period just prior to the Second World War, lies about four kilometers, or two-and-a-half miles further along. At this point, the road reaches the gates of the city of Abu Zenima (145.5 kilometers, or about ninety miles from the Tunnel), where one can find a gas station, a mechanic, and a few small stores

that allow one to stock up on basic provisions. Abu Zenima was a manufacturing center at the turn of the century; its industrial activity was chiefly linked to the presence of mineral processing plants for the exploitation of the manganese, copper, and chalk deposits found in the surrounding areas. From Abu Zenima (at two-and-a-half kilometers, or a mile-and-a-half from the gas station, to the south) one can take the track of Wadi Matalla; this is the easiest way to get to the site of Serabit el-Khadem (see itinerary). After travelling less than ten kilometers (about six miles) past Abu Zenima, there is an army checkpoint just about in line with a little oasis (154.5 kilometers, or about a hundred miles from the Tunnel) and with the ancient port of el-Markha (a name that derives from the Arabic word *maghara*, meaning "mine"), which was used during the time of the pharaohs for the transportation of the copper and turquoise found in the nearby mines in the region surrounding Serabit and Maghara. The road here crosses through the industrial center of Abu Rudeis (165.5 kilometers, or about a hundred five miles from the Tunnel), where there are oil refineries; the only possible reason to come to this town are the services that it offers (gas station, mechanic, post office, telephones, bank, stores). Immediately south of the city (about two kilometers, or a mile-and-a-half) begins a track that runs up Wadi Sidri and leads to the turquoise

28 right
At Hammam Musa, just before the city of el-Tor, a number of hot sulphur springs bubble forth, and the water is conducted to a number of tanks, in the shade of a great many palm trees.

28 top left
Two Beduin women as they soak in the water from the hot springs that emerge from the sand in the place known as Hammam Faraun Malun, "the pools of the cursed pharaoh," clearly a reference to the pharaoh that chased after the fleeing Hebrews, only to be destroyed, in the Biblical story, by the wrath of the Lord and the tumbling waters of the Red Sea.

28 center left
A major paved road runs along the west coast of the Sinai, connecting the Tunnel Ahmed Hamdi with the city of el-Tor.

28 bottom left
The limestone rocks of this region bear the signs of weather, erosion, and the ineluctable passage of time.

mines of Wadi Maghara. Lastly, one reaches the major intersection with the road that leads to Saint Catherine, and which runs the entire length of the majestic Wadi Feiran (see itinerary). In line with the intersection (202.5 kilometers, or a hundred twenty-seven miles from the Tunnel), one encounters a military checkpoint and a large coffee shop with a restaurant. Continuing along the main road and heading south, after a distance of fifty-six kilometers, or about thirty-five miles, one reaches the intersection with the road that leads to the oasis of Hammam Musa the "Baths of Moses," at the foot of Gebel Hammam Musa and at the

after about three kilometers (about two miles) one reaches the city of el-Tor, today the administrative capital of the southern Sinai. El-Tor takes its name from the Greek *to oros,* "the mountain"; the name was given by the earliest monks who settled here, with reference to the fact that here the mountainous region thrusts out to the sea. The old city of el-Tor originally sprang up around the bay, which served as a natural port with a strategic location at the mouth of the Gulf of Suez, allowing el-Tor to control the shipping trade to the north. When the winds were unfavorable, the ships that were having problems sailing up toward Suez would lay over at el-Tor, unloading their goods here for

29 These are two typical landscapes of the west coast of the Sinai: the soft limestones of the Tertiary Period, which make up the mountains of this region, show clear signs of erosion by the weather, while the high levels of clay located in the peneplain slow down the waters that run down from the highland, in some cases forming small oases.

mouth of Wadi el-Tor, where sulphurous thermal springs bubble up at a temperature of 27 degrees C; these warm springs tumble into a number of large pools, in the shade of magnificent palm trees. According to a number of scholars, Hammam Musa is the site of the Biblical place of *Elim,* mentioned in connection with its springs. In this site, the waters of which had therapeutic properties well known to the Beduin, the Khedive Abbas I had a palace built, of which nothing now remains, while Abbas' uncle and successor, Said Pasha, had the reservoir built which still today contains the waters of the springs. During the Eighties, Hammam Musa was transformed into a hot-spring spa, and the site was given its definitive appearance; unfortunately, since then, not a great deal of upkeep has been done, and this intriguing site now lies in a state of abandonment. Continuing along the main road, on the other hand,

shipment overland. El-Tor was an important point along the pilgrimage route to Mecca: here, a building had been erected to house those pilgrims who were obliged to spend the quarantine required. Near the port, a monastery was also built and dedicated to Saint James; this was an appendage of the Monastery of Saint Catherine, and is still active even now. The first monks settled here probably at the beginning of the fourth century, in the region around Wadi el-Tor, which was called *Reithou* in ancient times. Here in the sixth century the first monastery was built; the ruins of this construction were recently excavated and restored. After passing through the town of el-Tor, the road climbs toward the north, parallel to the coast of the Gulf of Eilat, at a few kilometers' distance. At a distance of one hundred ten kilometers, or about seventy miles, from el-Tor (four

hundred and fifty kilometers, or about two hundred and eighty miles, from the Tunnel A. H.), on the right, one sees the road that leads down to the National Park of Ras Mohammed, and after travelling another twenty kilometers (about twelve-and-a-half miles), one reaches the Egyptian army checkpoint at the entrance to Sharm el-Sheikh, where it is necessary to show one's passport. After passing through the Egyptian checkpoint, one encounters another checkpoint, this one manned by the MFO (one need not show his passport here), the road descends and skirts the bay of Sharm el-Sheikh, site of a port, and used by commercial and by military shipping, followed by an inlet called Sharm el-Maiya, used as a tourist marina, and the site of a great many hotels and diving centers, marking the boundary of the city of Sharm el-Sheikh.

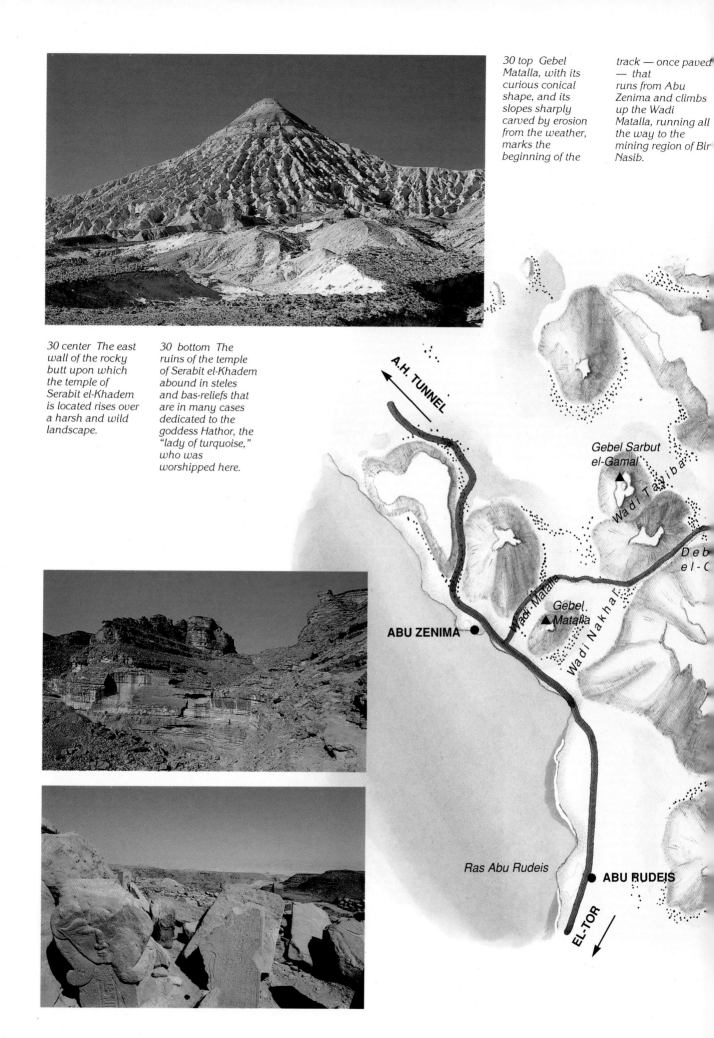

30 top Gebel Matalla, with its curious conical shape, and its slopes sharply carved by erosion from the weather, marks the beginning of the

track — once paved — that runs from Abu Zenima and climbs up the Wadi Matalla, running all the way to the mining region of Bir Nasib.

30 center The east wall of the rocky butt upon which the temple of Serabit el-Khadem is located rises over a harsh and wild landscape.

30 bottom The ruins of the temple of Serabit el-Khadem abound in steles and bas-reliefs that are in many cases dedicated to the goddess Hathor, the "lady of turquoise," who was worshipped here.

A.H. TUNNEL

Gebel Sarbut el-Gamal

Wadi Tayibat

Deb el-C

Wadi Matalla

Gebel Matalla

Wadi Nakhaf

ABU ZENIMA

Ras Abu Rudeis

ABU RUDEIS

EL-TOR

ebel Umm
inna ▲

Tomb of
Sheikh Habus

Barakat
encampment

HIGHLANDS EL-TÎH

W a d i E l - G e r f

Temple of
Serabit el-Khadem

Nasib ●

m ● ⚒
gma

Gebel Umm
Releigh ▲

Gebel Ghorabi ▲

Gebel
Serabit el-Khadem

W a d i K h a m i l a

W a d i S e j h

THE TEMPLE OF SERABIT EL-KHADEM AND THE TURQUOISE DEPOSITS

Two kilometers, or just over a mile, from the gas station at Abu Zenima, one can see on the left a little cut-off road, paved in the first part, heading east through Wadi Matalla, leading to the temple of Serabit el-Khadem. This is certainly the easiest route to Serabit which, along with the ruins of the city of Pelusium, constitutes one of the two most important archeological sites in the Sinai. One can reach the temple along this route even with a regular automobile, as opposed to an off-road vehicle, although toward the end of the drive the asphalt pavement gives way to an earth track that degenerates into stretches of sand. After passing the Gebel Matalla - the rock of which is a soft marly limestone of the Tertiary Period which present some very interesting forms of erosion - the road continues with no further turnings until it reaches a small pass; here it makes a sharp turn southward, and enters the Wadi Nasib. At this point the more difficult part of the trip begins, and the track runs along, alternately rocky and sandy. Keeping to one's left, it is necessary to stay on the track for a few kilometers, or miles, until one spots a small white Islamic building that stands atop a small hill. After travelling past this *sheikh*, as it is called by the locals, one encounters a number of houses of the Beduin who live in this place, the Barakat; these tribesmen live mainly on what they earn as hostelers and guides for passing tourists. From the Beduin camp, it is possible to reach the temple of Serabit el-Khadem by walking two different itineraries, one of which takes one to the temple from the west, the other from the east, both in about three hours. The best solution is that of taking a circular route, and planning to remain in the area for the entire day; it thus becomes possible to climb the eastern circle early in the morning, and then to climb down by the western side of the highland in the afternoon: this solution ensures that one will have good light the entire time, which is certainly a vital consideration if one wishes to examine the numerous and interesting bas-reliefs that one will find especially when climbing down on the western side. The temple of Serabit el-Khadem stands at an altitude of eight hundred fifty meters (about 2,800 feet) above sea level, on a highland that terminates in a massive rocky outcropping, bounded to the north by Wadi Sawik, to the west by Wadi Bata, to the east by Wadi Sarbout, to the southeast by Gebel Ghorabi (993 meters, or about 3,257 feet, above sea level) - this mountain is covered by a great dome of basalt - and lastly to the south by Gebel Serabit el-Khadem (1,096 meters, or about 3,595 feet, above sea level). Upon this promontory, which is made up of sandstone from the Devonian and the Upper Cretaceous, the uppermost layers of schist, rich in turquoise, practically outcrop to the surface. The turquoise mines are concentrated in a more-or-less circular area, with a diameter of 1.2 kilometers (three-quarters of a mile) to the southwest of the temple:

it is possible to see a number of galleries, shafts, and tunnels, with inscriptions dating for the most part from the Middle Kingdom, even though the Egyptians continued to work the mines much later.
In particular, the inscriptions date from the era of Amenemhat II (years 17 and 24 of his reign), Amenemhat III, and Tuthmosis IV. Another very important group of large mines, dating from the Twelfth Dynasty, can be found northwest of the temple, in the area around Wadi Dhaba, and on the left-hand side of the wadi itself. On the western side of the highland, but on the opposite slope of the highland, overlooking Wadi Bata, there is also a small chapel dug out of the living rock, and dating from the New Kingdom. The temple, located on the northeastern side of the highland, extends over two hundred meters (six hundred fifty feet) of ground. It was built with the manpower of Semite laborers (probably semi-nomadic local tribesmen, associated with the

32 This picture offers an overall view of the temple of Serabit el-Khadem, which stands on a highland rising to an altitude of 850 meters, or 2,788 feet.

33 A piece of rough turquoise found in the region of Serabit shows the precious beauty of this mineral.

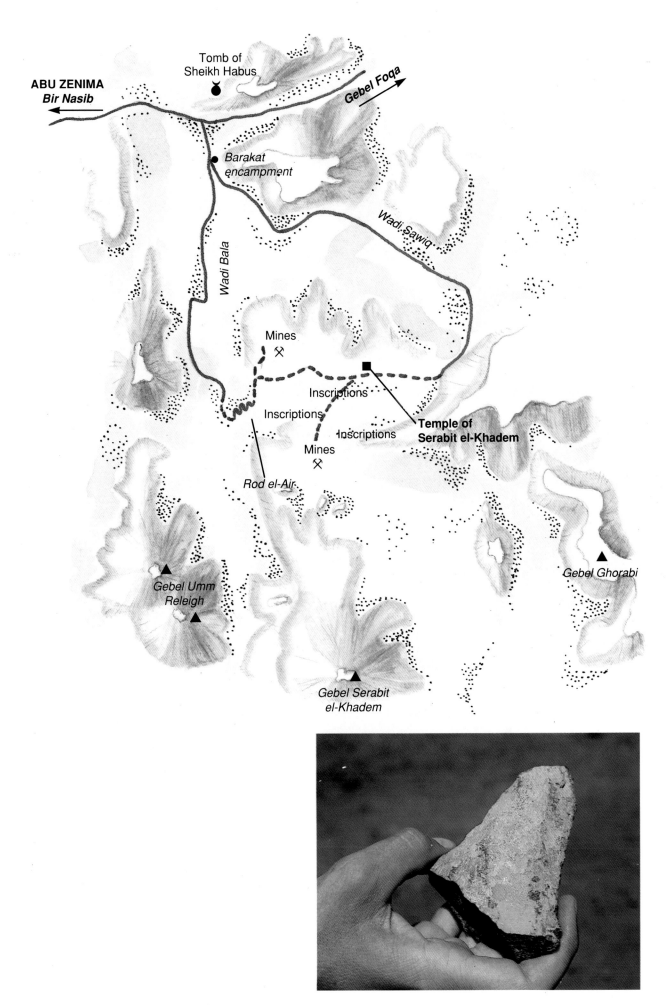

ABU ZENIMA
Bir Nasib

Tomb of
Sheikh Habus

Gebel Foqa

Barakat
encampment

Wadi Bala

Wadi Sawiq

Mines

Inscriptions

Inscriptions

Inscriptions

Mines

Rod el-Air

Temple of
Serabit el-Khadem

Gebel Umm
Releigh

Gebel Ghorabi

Gebel Serabit
el-Khadem

Aamu Arabs or the Retennu Syrians), during the reigns of the pharaohs of the Twelfth Dynasty, on a Semitic cultural sites where it is believed that a local deity - "Lord of the Eastern Desert" and "Lord of the foreign Lands" - was worshipped. At first, during the Twelfth Dynasty, the temple was formed by a rock-cut chapel dedicated to the goddess Hathor; later other rooms were added and dedicated to Sopdu. New and impressive works of expansion were then undertaken, during the period of the Eighteenth Dynasty, when a long series of halls in a line were built, giving the temple its modern-day appearance. The two final halls (the ones farthest to the west) were added during the Ramesside period, and Ramesses VI is the latest name of a pharaoh documented here. In the temple and all around it, in the highest points of the highland and in a range of four hundred meters (thirteen hundred feet) all around it, a great number of steles (some of them taller than two meters, or six-and-a-half feet), with inscriptions on all four of their faces, bearing spells and religious invocations and accounts of mining expeditions: among the largest steles, there is one that dates back to the time of Sethos I. The site of Serabit el-Khadem (which reached its peak of importance during the Twelfth Dynasty, when turquoise mining was done alongside the mining and smelting of copper in the nearby Wadi Nasib) was excavated in the early years of the century by the celebrated archeologist William Flinders Petrie. Petrie, who was also responsible for the publication of most of the steles and inscriptions on the site (see F. Petrie, *Researches in Sinai*, 1906), showed, on the basis of the artifacts uncovered, that in the temple of Serabit el-Khadem the ancient Egyptians and Semites had practiced together the same cults and religions and that, therefore, the quarrying and mining had not been carried out by slaves or prisoners, but by local manpower or by freed Semitic laborers, whose leader was described as the "brother of the prince of Retennu."

PLAN OF THE TEMPLE OF SERABIT EL-KHADEM ACCORDING TO FLINDERS PETRIE

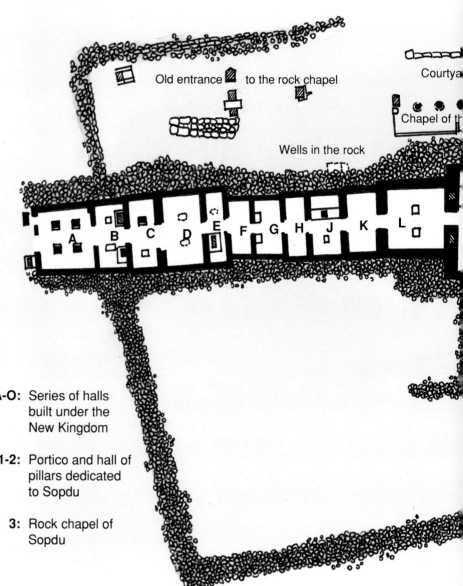

Old entrance to the rock chapel

Courtya

Chapel of th

Wells in the rock

A B C D E F G H J K L

A-O: Series of halls built under the New Kingdom

1-2: Portico and hall of pillars dedicated to Sopdu

3: Rock chapel of Sopdu

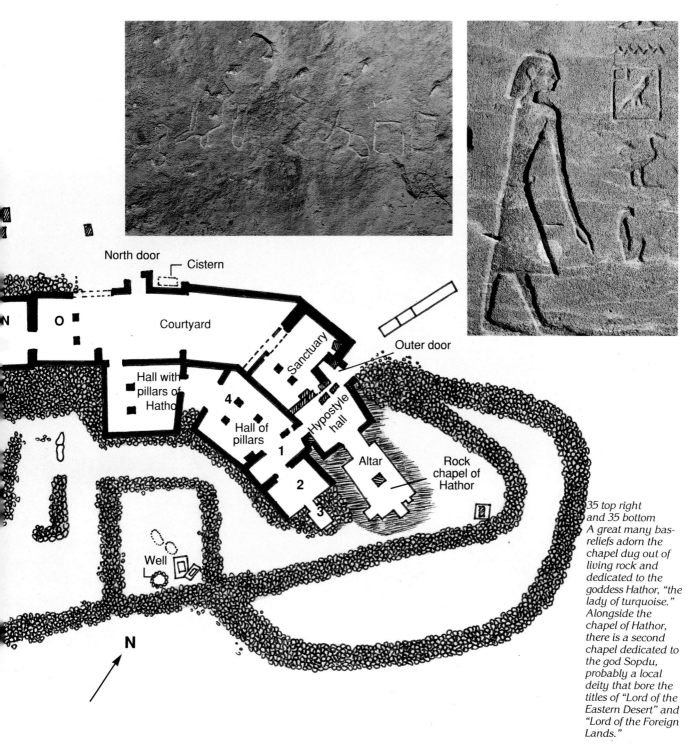

North door

Cistern

Courtyard

Sanctuary

N

O

Outer door

Hall with pillars of Hathor

Hypostyle hall

4

Hall of pillars

1

Altar

Rock chapel of Hathor

2

3

Well

N

35 top right and 35 bottom
A great many bas-reliefs adorn the chapel dug out of living rock and dedicated to the goddess Hathor, "the lady of turquoise." Alongside the chapel of Hathor, there is a second chapel dedicated to the god Sopdu, probably a local deity that bore the titles of "Lord of the Eastern Desert" and "Lord of the Foreign Lands."

34 Those who climb up to the temple of Serabit el-Khadem from the western side, in the site that the Beduins call Rod el-Air, can observe a great many rock carvings: this particular one shows an Egyptian ship with features that date it from the New Kingdom.

35 top left
On the walls of the mines located near the temple of Serabit el-Khadem, in 1906, the renowned Egyptologist, Sir William Flinders Petrie found strange carvings that were at first sight incomprehensible: by studying them at length, he found that these were the earliest forms of a Semitic alphabetical system, now known as "protosinaitic."

THE REGION OF SERABIT EL-KHADEM - BIR NASIB

The region that extends around the temple of Serabit el-Khadem can provide a number of excursions of particular interest, although one certainly will need a four-wheel drive vehicle, and, more important, the assistance of a local Bedouin guide. Setting out from the small Bedouin settlement where the family of the Barakat live, the most interesting excursion involves a visit to the ancient mining sites of Bir Nasib and of the Wadi Kharig. Returning along the track for a number of kilometers or miles, one reaches Serabit from Abu Zenima, along all that survives of the old paved road built to transport manganese ores; then one must turn left and head southeast, following the Wadi Nasib for three-and-a-half kilometers (two miles). This brings one along a very easy and well-marked track to the small oasis of Bir Nasib, where enormous quantities of blackish slag (the quantity has been estimated to be one hundred thousand tons) bear witness to what was once the most important mining site during the time of the pharaohs. There were the furnaces that were used in smelting the copper ores that were extracted from the surrounding region, especially in the nearby Wadi Kharig. Mining here began as early as the Old Kingdom, but especially during the Middle and

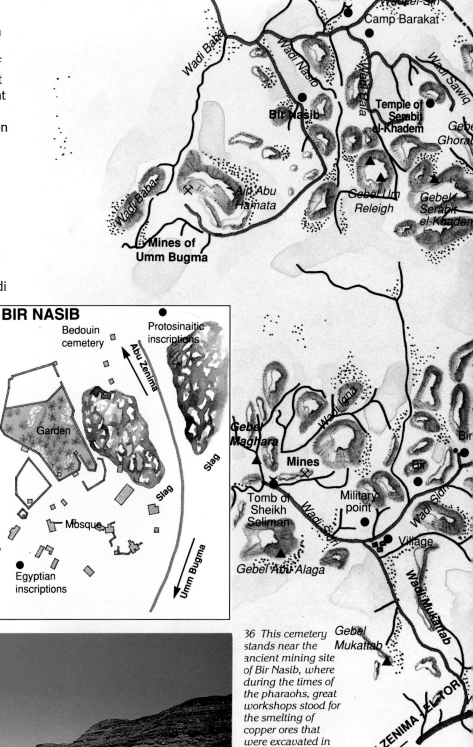

36 This cemetery stands near the ancient mining site of Bir Nasib, where during the times of the pharaohs, great workshops stood for the smelting of copper ores that were excavated in the surrounding region.

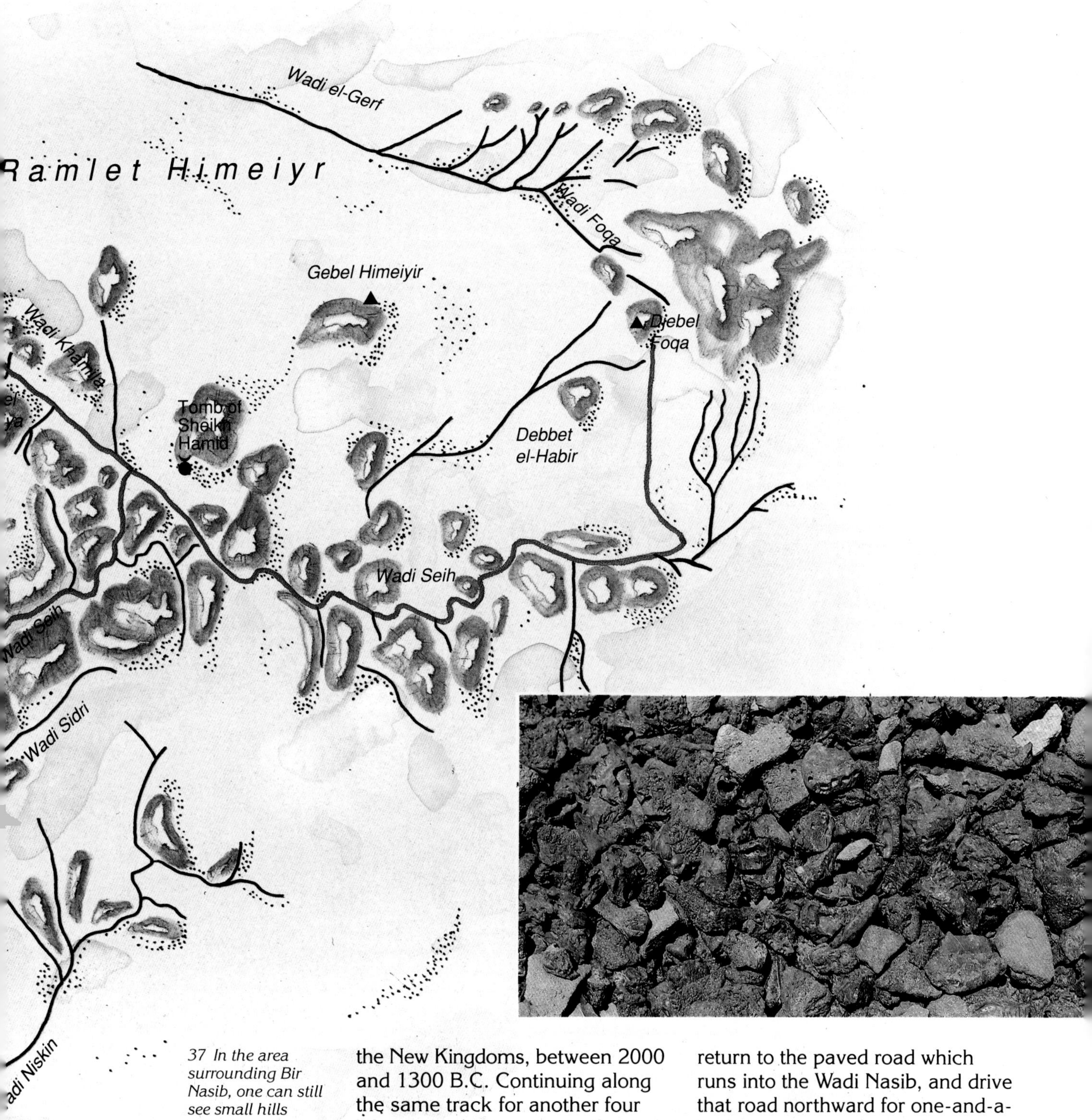
Wadi el-Gerf
Ramlet Himeiyr
Wadi Foqa
Gebel Himeiyir
Wadi Khamila
Djebel Foqa
Tomb of Sheikh Hamid
Debbet el-Habir
Wadi Seih
Wadi Seih
Wadi Sidri
adi Niskin
Oase of Feiran

37 *In the area surrounding Bir Nasib, one can still see small hills which represent slagheaps from the smelting of copper ores. In order to have some idea of the volume of production of copper in Sinai during the times of the pharaohs, suffice it to consider that an estimate of the volume of the slag still remaining in Bir Nasib amounts to some one hundred thousand tons.*

the New Kingdoms, between 2000 and 1300 B.C. Continuing along the same track for another four kilometers (two-and-a-half miles), one reaches a large mine, which is still being worked to some extent for the extraction of manganese ore. From here, it is possible to reach the great manganese mine of Umm Bugma, along a very difficult track, at a distance of about fifteen kilometers (about ten miles), leaving Gebel Marahil on one's left, and turning from here westward, along the Wadi Shellal. If one wishes to visit the ancient mines of the Wadi Kharig, then one must return to the paved road which runs into the Wadi Nasib, and drive that road northward for one-and-a-half kilometers (one mile), until one reaches the very difficult track that runs southwest along the Wadi Baba. After four kilometers (two-and-a-half miles), one can see on the right the confluence with the Wadi Kharig, which runs northward and can be driven for a short stretch. Then one must park one's car and continue on foot in order to visit the ancient mines on the walls of which one can still clearly see the marks left by the tools used by laborers during the time of the pharaohs.

WADI FEIRAN

If one takes the road at the major intersection preceded by a sign which reads, "St. Katherine," at a distance of two hundred and seven kilometers (one hundred and twenty-nine miles) from the Tunnel A.H., along the road that leads to el-Tor and to el-Sharm el Sheikh, one climbs up the Wadi Feiran, one of the largest and most important wadis in the entire Sinai Peninsula, which runs from the coast of the Gulf of Suez directly to the Monastery of Saint Catherine. At its beginning this wadi, which abounds in Biblical monuments and sites, is broad and

sandy and the road winds, climbing slightly uphill while the landscape changes, becoming progressively more mountainous and wild. After travelling 22.5 kilometers (fourteen miles) from the intersection, on the left one will see - in line with the mouth of Wadi Gharuel - the beginning of the track (not marked) which leads to Wadi Maghara, to the Wadi Mukattab, and finally, to Serabit el-Khadem. A little further along, the paved road runs alongside a rock that the Bedouins call Hesi el-Khattatin, a place-name that means, the "Spring Hidden by the Scribes." The origin of this odd

place-name (which makes reference to Moses and Aaron whom the local population considers to be the scribes par excellence) is linked to a Bedouin tradition which holds that this is the rock that Moses struck with his rod, making a spring of pure fresh water leap forth for his people (see Exodus 17). After travelling forty-three kilometers (twenty-seven miles) past the intersection, one begins to see the first palm trees and tamarisks along the wadi, in line with the small Oasis of Khessuah, adjacent to the larger Oasis of Feiran, a necessary overnight stay for all those pilgrims who were on their way to the

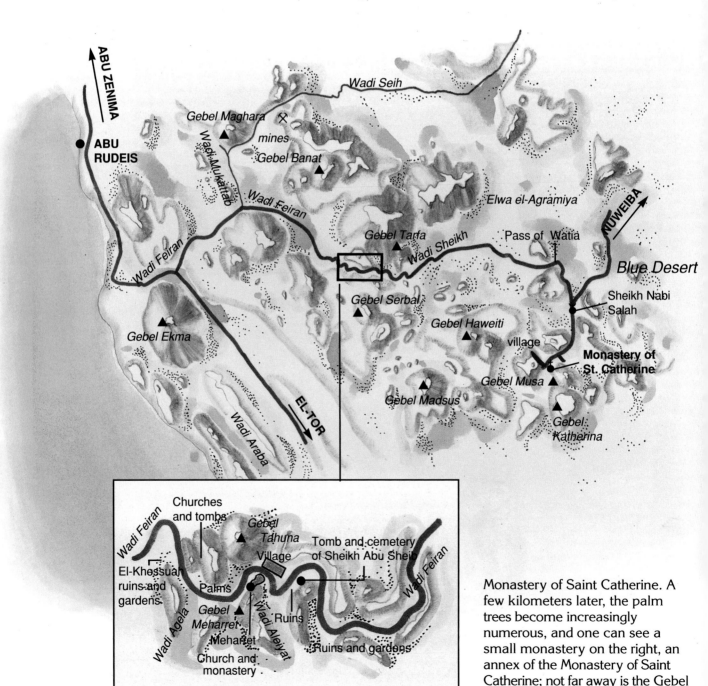

Monastery of Saint Catherine. A few kilometers later, the palm trees become increasingly numerous, and one can see a small monastery on the right, an annex of the Monastery of Saint Catherine; not far away is the Gebel Meharret and a vast archeological

area, where digs have unearthed a great many churches, then comes the tiny village of Ferian and, on the other side of the wadi, Gebel Tahuna, which looms up over the largest grove of palm trees in the entire Sinai Peninsula. On the summit of the Gebel a cross has been erected. According to the itinerary of Exodus, the oasis of Feiran is considered to be the true site of *Rafidim* (see Exodus 17) where the Hebrews made their encampment and where a battle was fought with the Amalecites. The battle ended with a victory for the Hebrews under their general Joshua, while Moses prayed for his people on the nearby mountain, supposedly none other than Gebel Tahuna. On the slopes of this mountain, one can still see the ruins of a church built to commemorate the battle, and the ruins of other churches dedicated to Hur and Aaron. The first church was also mentioned in the account by the nun Aeteria of her travels; she had undertaken a pilgrimage to the Monastery of Saint Catherine in the fourth century A.D. In this period, Feiran was an important center, and many monks and anchorites had taken up residence in the surrounding area. It had become the seat of a bishopric. The city, which had been fortified, stretched out at the foot of Gebel Tahuna, while the cathedral and other churches stood near the present convent, on the slopes of the hill of el-Meharret; the city ruins have been excavated by the German Archeological Institute. The bishop of Feiran was subordinate to the patriarch of Jerusalem, and originally held sway over the Monastery of Saint Catherine, until the time of the Nestorian heresy, when there was a split between Feiran and the Monastery of Saint Catherine; in fact, the bishop of Feiran had joined the ranks of the Nestorians, and was deposed in the seventh century by the Council of Constantinople. The bishop's functions were taken over by the convent of Saint Catherine, whose monks had remained faithful to the orthodox doctrines. Following this episode, the city of Feiran slowly dwindled and then fell into ruins. It never

recovered from this abandonment, and many of the architectural features of the churches of the city were recycled in the construction of the monastery. After passing by the modern-day village of Feiran, which lies in the eastern section of the oasis, one can see a small cemetery on the right and the tomb of Sheikh Abu Sheib: many gardens adorn both edges of the wadi, and the vegetation is characterized by a great many tamarisks. Along the walls of the wadi, in this area, one can see lacustrine earth sediments, the remains of a lake. In ancient times major rains had caused the formation of a lake basin that had been closed off downstream by a landslide that extended, walling off the area between Gebel Meharret and Gebel Tahuna. The lacustrine deposits then give way to formations of dikes, which work their way in amongst the colored rocks, made up of gneiss, corresponding with the mouth of the Wadi el-Akhdar. After

joining up with the Wadi el-Akhdar, the road runs through a narrow stretch some ten meters (thirty feet) in length, called el-Bueib. After passing through this sort of natural gate, the Wadi Feiran ends and the Wadi el-Sheikh begins, and can be considered a sort of continuation of the first one. This takes one to the small verdant Oasis of Tarfat ("the tamarisks"), adorned with numerous gardens of palm trees, acacias, fruit trees, and tamarisks. After passing the oasis, one drives through the Watia Pass (eighty-five kilometers, or fifty-three miles, past the fork in the road), a gorge several hundred meters (yards) in length, which runs between tall granite cliffs only about thirty meters (a hundred feet) apart at their narrowest. After skirting around the mountain bulk of Gebel Freiah, one reaches a military checkpoint and the intersection with the road that connects Nuweiba with Saint Catherine, in line with the tomb of Sheikh Nabi Salah.

39 top
The archeological area of Gebel Meharret, behind the modern-day convent, testifies to the importance of Feiran prior to the construction of the Monastery of St. Catherine. Excavations have unearthed the remains of the numerous churches of Feiran, built when the city was the see of the bishop of the Sinai.

39 center
An overall view of the Wadi Feiran and its immense palm grove, the largest in all of the Sinai. It was at Feiran, identified as the Biblical site of Rafidim, that, according to tradition, that the great battle took place between the Hebrews and the Amaleciti.

39 bottom
The small nunnery that lies in the Wadi Feiran is an annex of the Monastery of St. Catherine.

WADI MUKATTAB - WADI MAGHARA - GEBEL FUGA

40 top In this panoramic view, it is possible to see the Gebel Maghara, in the center. Along the slopes of this mountain lay the ancient turquoise mines, worked under the pharaohs ever since the Third Dynasty.

40 center A small rocky cone stands alone above the sands of the region known as Ramlet Himeiyr: on its side, one can see a strange local phenomenon on the rock that, through the action of the ferrous oxides, is colored bright red.

40 bottom The columns of lava that emerge from the sandstone of Gebel Fuga, at a place known as the "Forest of Columns," constitute one of the most intriguing geological oddities in the Sinai.

If one takes the track that splits off from the paved road running through Wadi Feiran, at a distance of 22.5 kilometers (fourteen miles) from the intersection with the road that links the Tunnel A.H. with el-Tor, then one will climb the Wadi Mukattab, a place-name that means "Valley of the Scriptures." After travelling about six kilometers (four miles) along the left side of the wadi, one begins to see the rock graffiti that characterize this wadi, extending over a distance of three kilometers (two miles). The graffiti largely date from the time of the Nabataeans, and date back from between the second and the third century A.D.,

although there are also carvings dating from the Roman or Byzantine eras. After touring the site, one continues to climb up the Wadi Mukattab, and then one reaches the intersection with the large Wadi Sidri. At this point, if one should wish to tour the ancient turquoise mines of the Wadi Maghara (a place-name that means "Valley of Mines"), then one must follow the left-hand track and continue in a northwesterly direction, until reaching the tomb of Sheikh Soliman. At this point, one should follow the right-hand track and enter the Wadi Maghara and, after a kilometer (half a mile), one reaches the head of this little valley, which splits up into Wadi Iqna on the right and Wadi Qenaia on the left. It is in this second wadi that one can find the turquoise mines: at this point it is necessary to park the four-wheel drive vehicle and to continue making one's way for another couple of hundred meters (yards), climbing the eastern slope of Gebel Maghara which is equivalent to the left-hand slope of the wadi. One can thus tour the mines dug out into the side of the mountain. Here one can also see a celebrated bas-relief dating from the Old Kingdom, depicting king Sekhemkhet (Third Dynasty, about 2600 B.C.), standing beside a dignitary identified as the "prince, commander of the expedition"; this bas-relief was uncovered by the British explorer Palmer in 1868. The British Egyptologist William Flinders Petrie, who was responsible for the first systematic exploration of the Sinai peninsula at the turn of the century, found no fewer than twelve bas-reliefs in this wadi, executed between the First and the Eighteenth Dynasties; these bas-reliefs were later damaged by misguided attempts to mine the region. They were in part detached and transported to the Cairo Museum. In ancient times, a track - which can still be used - connected the mines of Maghara with the port of Markha in the Gulf of Suez (eight kilometers or five miles, south of Abu Zenima) where the turquoise and copper - brought down from Maghara, Serabit and the Wadi Kharig - were loaded onto ships that sailed off with it to Egypt. This track, which sets out from Sheikh Soliman, runs northwes along the Wadi Budra, and then cuts off into the Wadi Baba, which opens out onto the coastal plain of el-Markha. After touring the site, it is necessary to travel back to the intersection with the Wadi Sidri, to climb the wadi which extends into the Wadi Sheikh, as far as the tomb of Sheikh Hamid. From this intersection, it is possible:

a) head southeast, running along the Wadi Labwa and the Wadi El-Akhdar, and reaching the paved road that runs from Feiran to Saint Catherine (some forty kilometers or twenty-five miles);

b) head northwest and travel to Serabit el-Khadem, a distance of thirty-eight kilometers or twenty-four miles, along the Wadi Khamila. If one enters the winding track that heads northeast, one reaches a vast sandy plateau that the Bedouins call Ramlet Himeiyir, with rocky formations made up of reddish sandstone, in some cases polychrome, and here one can see one of the most remarkable geological curiosities in the entire Sinai peninsula: Gebel Fuga, also known with the name of "Forest of Pillars." The name comes from the

ARRANGEMENT OF THE BAS-RELIEFS IN THE WADI MAGHARA

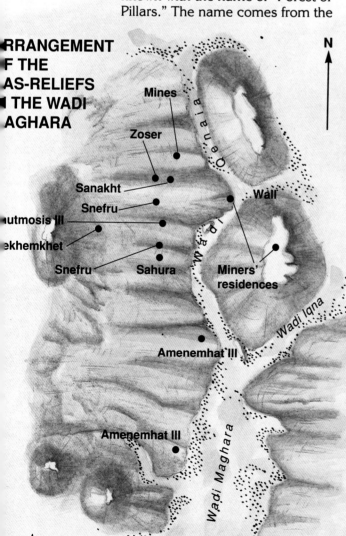

Mines

Zoser

Sanakht

Snefru

Thutmosis III

Sekhemkhet

Snefru

Sahura

Wali

Miners' residences

Amenemhat III

Amenemhat III

Wadi Maghara

Wadi Iqna

Qenaia

N

tubular columns of black lava there are driven up like many stalagmites from the surrounding rock, made up reddish-yellow sandstones. This itinerary, running from the Wadi Maghara to Gebel Fuga, is about fifty-five kilometers (thirty-four miles) in length (driving time, about three hours), and is an interesting itinerary in terms of naturalistic features. Unfortunately, the track includes many difficult passages and, most important, there are no markings or indications to show one the way to this formation. One must bring a guide, therefore. From Gebel Fuga, it is possible to reach the region of Serabit el-Khadem, by following a sandy track that runs along a broad arc through the expanse of Ramlet Himeiyir, finally reaching the area around Serabit el-Khadem via Sheikh Habus.

41 The Wadi Mukattab, a place name that means "valley of inscriptions," is adorned with a great many graffiti, largely dating from Nabatean times, although there are quite a few Roman and Byzantine inscriptions as well.

42 top At the center of this panoramic view of Ras Mohammed, one can see the deep waters of Hidden Bay, with the nearby Mangrove Island, and its channel.

42 center
The monumental entrance gate to the National Park of Ras Mohammed is made of reinforced cement, and is the work of an Egyptian artist.

42 bottom
The entrance to the National Park of Ras Mohammed is marked by two small, conical structures made of stone.

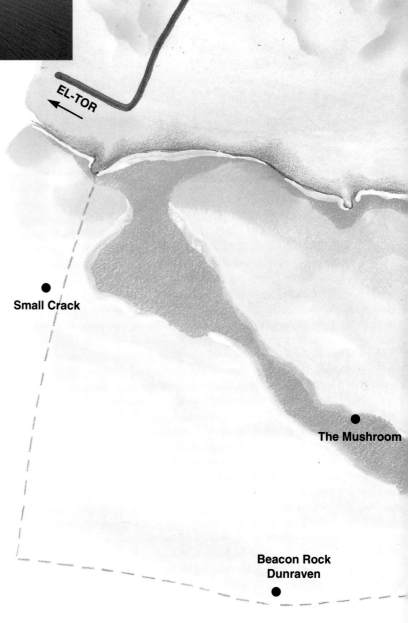

EL-TOR

Small Crack

The Mushroom

**Beacon Rock
Dunraven**

Map labels

SHARM EL-SHEIKH

Ras Umm Sidd

Entrance and ticket booth

Visitor's center and coffee shop

Marsa Ghazlani

Educational diving itinerary

Ras Ghazlani

Ras Ghazlani

Marsa Bareika

Marsa Bareika

onumental
te

Ras Atar

Ras Atar

rnative reef

Ras Mohammed

The Quay

Hidden Bay

43 The modern Visitors' Center, built inside the park, not only features a coffee shop, but also a lecture room and an auditorium, where the rangers deliver brief introductory talks about the park, projecting slides and documentaries.

RAS MOHAMMED

The peninsula of Ras Mohammed is located at the southern extremity of the Sinai, at a distance of about twenty kilometers (twelve-and-a-half miles) by land and eight kilometers (five miles) by sea. This is an unspoiled site of remarkable beauty and of exceptional interest in terms of nature and wildlife; it was declared a National Park in 1983. The park includes a surface area that is far greater than the peninsula itself, and is protected and placed under a number of legislative and naturalistic restrictions that ensure its inviolability. A number of rangers - unfortunately, not as many as the park needs - work throughout the park territory in pursuit of four tasks and purposes:
1. providing information and education to the visitors through campaigns of consensus-formation, seminars, and publications;
2. explanation of the purposes of the park to the Beduins, so that they can help to properly manage their own land;
3. scientific research and environmental monitoring;
4. oversight of visitors to ensure that they respect the laws designed to protect the natural heritage.
A series of well-marked routes within the park's bounds (one cannot wander off these itineraries) allow the visitor to discover all of the beauty of the site by land, while, for those who wish to explore the magnificent seabeds by arriving by water, there are a number of places where one can dive. In order to get to know the area well, it is best to make both tours, because there is a close bond between the marine ecosystem and its dry-land counterpart, or, to be more exact, among five different ecosystems: desert, lagoon, coast, coral and marine.

TOPOGRAPHY AND GEOLOGY OF THE PARK OF RAS MOHAMMED

In its southernmost section, the Park of Ras Mohammed is made up of a rocky promontory, linked to the mainland by a peninsula that extends for some three-and-a-half kilometers (just over two miles) in length, and is about a kilometer (just over half a mile) in width. This peninsula juts southward into the Red Sea, between the Gulf of Suez, with an average depth of no more than a hundred meters (three hundred thirty feet), and the Gulf of Eilat, with a depth that plunges to close to two thousand meters (6,560 feet). This enormous morphological difference is due to the fact that the Gulf of Eilat is the beginning of the enormous cleavage in the earth's crust that separated the two great continental plates of Africa and Eurasia during the Tertiary Period. The peninsula of Ras Mohammed is split up into two rocky spits of land separated by a deep bay called Hidden Bay. The western section presents two deep fissures in its center, while on the southeastern side it is flanked by a low and sandy islet called the Mangroves Island, from which it is separated by a shallow channel that runs from northwest to southeast, called the Mangroves Canal. The eastern section runs parallel with the western section, and terminates in a small bay, called Shark Observatory Bay, whose easternmost point constitutes the promontory of Ras Mohammed, which rises about sixty meters (almost two hundred feet) above sea level. Upon its summit is the Shark Observatory, made up of three observation terraces, high above the waters of the Red Sea. In geological terms, the peninsula of Ras Mohammed is constituted by a fossil coral reef that emerged during the Quaternary Period, about seventy-

44 top
The promontory of Ras Mohammed and the Main Beach: the promontory, which rises some fifty meters, or a hundred fifty feet, is
formed from a fossil coral reef; on the summit, a little observation platform has been placed, and called the "Shark Observatory."

44 bottom
This little beach, which runs along the coast not far from Ras Mohammed, is known as "Eel Garden," inasmuch
as there is a colony of sea eels (Gorgasia sillneri) that lives in the seabeds here, at a depth of about fifteen meters, or fifty feet.

five thousand years ago, as a result of profound changes in the coastline, caused by huge variations in sea levels around the planet, these variations were in turn caused by the onset and end of the great ice ages. In the northernmost area of the Park, there are large formations of sand dunes; there are major alluvial soil deposits consisting of rough conglomerates that correspond to wadis that bear runoff from the mountainous areas lying to the north; outcroppings of Miocene limestone, with an array of fossil fauna ranging from gastropods, lamellibranches, and fragments of echinoderms all the way to corals, of course. Found alongside these older limestones are magmatic rocks belongin to the group of granitoids (granodiorites and granites).

This great heterogeneity of rock formations underlies the abundance and vast array of ecosystems that so strongly distinguishes the Park of Ras Mohammed.

FAUNA AND FLORA

The waters that surround the Park are distinguished by the presence of an imposing system of coral reefs that entirely surround the head of the promontory and extend along its coasts, which are in turn some forty-to-fifty percent formed of fossil coral formations. The coral reefs have a terraced configuration along the coast, terracings that maintain an average depth of twelve to fifteen meters (forty to fifty feet) and then drop away in steep subaqueous scarps to depths of from seventy to a hundred meters (two hundred thirty to three hundred thirty feet). There are also a great number of small and mid-sized coral reefs, which rise from fairly shallow seabeds. This high concentration of coral in the area around Ras Mohammed naturally corresponds to a remarkable variety of underwater life, in which the leading characters are: *Millepora sp.* - *Millepora dicotoma* is often also called "fire corals" - *Acropora sp.*, *Favia sp.*, *Favites sp.*, *Porites sp.*, *Fungia sp.* and *Dendronephtya*. Among the lamellibranches, the imposing Tridacnidae (*Tridacna maxima*) are quite common. The rich abundance of fishlife, both reef and pelagic fish, includes over a thousand species, some of which are endemic, which is to say, common only to the Red Sea. This degree of endemicity exists in relation to the degree to which this sea basin has been isolated, through tectonic phenomena that caused a temporary lifting of the seabeds in the southernmost area, probably at the beginning of the Quarternary Period.
Among the most common types of fish let us first mention the humphead wrasse (*Cheilinus undulatus*) which can generally be found in the areas around the reef, marked by its remarkably sociable nature as far as scuba divers are concerned; then there are snappers *(Lutjanus bohar)*, that live in large schools and are particularly prized as good eating; the turkeyfish (*Pterois volitans*);

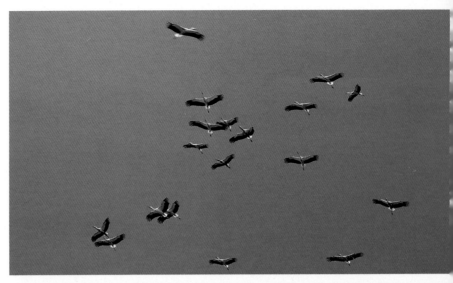

the coral grouper (*Cephalopholis miniata*); and the eels (*Gorgasia sillneri*). There are many types of sharks as well in the waters of Ras Mohammed; among them are the whitetip reef shark (*Trinaenodon obesus*), the blacktip reef shark (*Carcharhinus melanopterus*), and the shortnose blacktail shark (*Carcharhinus wheeleri*). All of these sharks are relatively small in size (they rarely grow to be much longer than one-and-a-half meters, or about five feet). In the springtime especially, one can run into large hammerhead sharks (*Sphyrna lewini*), which are ocean bottom-dwellers. Along the beaches and close-in to the coast, live a number of sea turtles, including the green sea turtle (*Chelonia mydas*). As far as the park's flora is concerned, we can report that some kind of mangrovers flourishes greatly, and plays an important role in preserving the coastal ecosystem (see Park of Nabq).

46 top The sky over Ras Mohammed is enlivened by the majestic flight of a group of storks.

46 center Along the coastline of Ras Mohammed in some places the sand dunes run right down to the water.

46 bottom The area around Ras Mohammed is one of the main stopover areas for storks.

47 top left Large sea fans, brightened by the intense shades of the stupendous alcyonarians, stand out sharply against the surface of the sea.

47 top right A small clownfish (Amphiprion bicinctus), inquisitive about the presence of the photographer, ventures away from the sea anemone that is hosting the fish.

The land fauna includes many mammals, such as gazelles, wild goats (*Ibex sp.*), foxes (*Vulpes rueppelli and Vulpes zerda*), and small rodents. Of particular importance are the many species of birds that either have territory here or who pass through during their migrations. Ras Mohammed is in fact a point of enormous importance in the migratory itineraries of storks (*Ciconia ciconia*); these birds leave Northern Europe and head for Africa, either flying across the Strait of Gibraltar, or else over Turkey and the Sinai. About twenty-thousand storks fly over the Sinai each year between April and May, and between September and October, and among their favorite stopover stations ar the parks of Ras Mohammed and Nabq. Among the other species of birds found here, let us mention the osprey (*Pandion haliaetus*) and the cinereous gull (*Larus hemprichii*).

47 center The seabeds of Ras Mohammed are among the most spectacular and lush in the Red Sea. On the right in this picture one can see the Shark Observatory, which rises fifty-five meters, or one hundred eighty feet, above the surface of the sea.

47 bottom When diving at Ras Mohammed it is exceedingly common to encounter specimens of the humphead wrasse (Cheilinus undulatus); they generally show no fear, and allow scuba divers to approach quite close.

Land routes

After entering through the front gate and ticket office made up of two small pyramid-shaped structures, the asphalt road heads off in a southeastern direction, toward the bay of Marsa Ghazlani. The track that cuts away from the road, on the left, at a distance of 2.8 kilometers, or about one-and-three-quarters of a mile past the front gate, leads to the Visitors' Center, which is reached about one-and-a-half kilometers, or about a mile further on. Just after the track begins, there is another route that branches off to the right; this leads directly to the beach of Marsa Ghazlani where a sign indicates the beginning of the educational underwater itinerary that follows the reef along the southern portion of the bay, with plaques bearing information on the various types of coral formations. The itinerary can be undertaken with just a mask and snorkel.

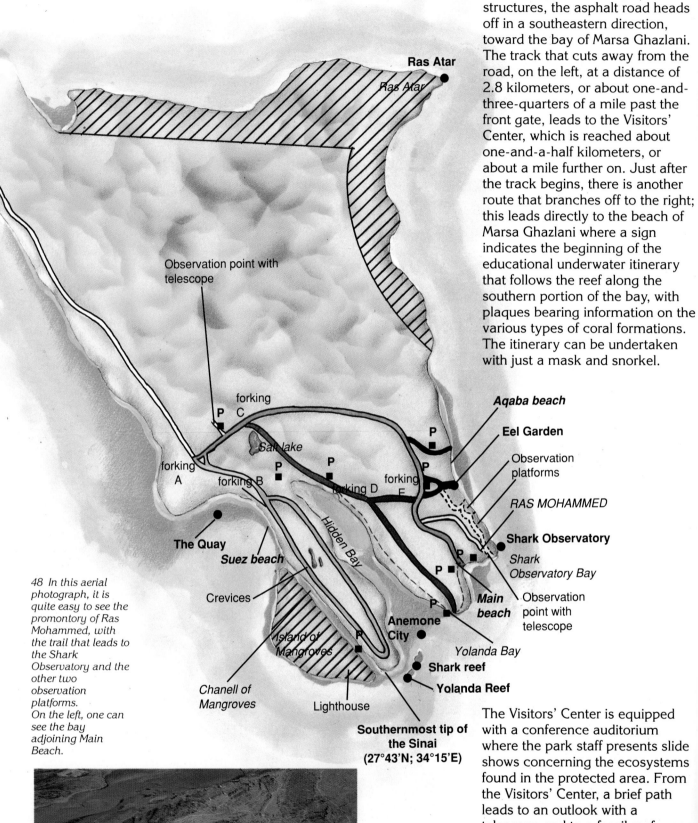

Ras Atar

Ras Atar

Observation point with telescope

forking C

Salt lake

forking A

forking B

The Quay

Suez beach

Crevices

forking D

Hidden Bay

Island of Mangroves

Chanell of Mangroves

Lighthouse

P

Aqaba beach

Eel Garden

Observation platforms

RAS MOHAMMED

forking E

Shark Observatory

Shark Observatory Bay

Observation point with telescope

Main beach

Anemone City

Yolanda Bay

Shark reef

Yolanda Reef

Southernmost tip of the Sinai (27°43'N; 34°15'E)

48 In this aerial photograph, it is quite easy to see the promontory of Ras Mohammed, with the trail that leads to the Shark Observatory and the other two observation platforms. On the left, one can see the bay adjoining Main Beach.

49 top The eastern coast of the peninsula of Ras Mohammed, seen here from Aqaba Beach, is washed by the warm waters of the Red Sea.

The Visitors' Center is equipped with a conference auditorium where the park staff presents slide shows concerning the ecosystems found in the protected area. From the Visitors' Center, a brief path leads to an outlook with a telescope and to a fossil reef, upon which it is possible to observe the principal forms of coral. Continuing along the asphalt road, which makes a wide curve toward the southwest, and then heads due south, one then passes on the left - at a distance of eight kilometers, or about five miles, from the front gate - the Center of Operations for the park personnel, equipped with a research center, laboratories, and technical services of all sorts. From this center, located on the eastern side of the bay of Marsa Bareka, a track begins that follows the coast, runs by a military checkpoint, and leads on to a number of small bays where the camping areas are indicated (one can only camp with the prior approval of the park authorities). The asphalt road now runs through a series of splendid dunes which run right down to the water's edge; the sand of these dunes sometimes covers the road. The road now reaches the slope of the peninsula of Ras Mohammed, which juts out into the Gulf of Suez. Then the road runs through the monumental gate (at a distance of 12.4 kilometers, or about eight miles past the front gate), designed and built in reinforced concrete by the Egyptian artist Ali Azzam. The road continues to run parallel with the coast on a sandy terrain and, just where the road curves to the west, it gives way to a track (at a distance of 15.8 kilometers, or about ten miles past the front gate). After about three hundred meters (about three hundred thirty feet), one reaches the first fork in the road (intersection A), where one can select between two different routes, respectively to the east and to the west of the deep inlet known as Hidden Bay, whose clear vibrant blue waters contrast with the golden sand that surrounds them. The tracks, which correspond with various routes, are marked by different colors: green, purple, red, blue, yellow, and black.

A Route 1

From intersection A one heads south, taking the right-hand track, marked with the color green, and one reaches a second fork in the road (intersection B), where a circular route begins, running around the western section of the Hidden Bay. Just beyond the fork in the road, on the right, a heap of rocks tumbled into the sea mark the diving site known as "The Quay." Follow the right-hand track and continue past the Suez Beach,

while on the left one can glimpse the northernmost portion of the Hidden Bay.

At a distance of about seven hundred meters (or about 2,300 feet) past intersection B, there is a little track that leads to a pair of menacing-looking crevices caused by seismic phenomena; rocks on the ground warn passersby of the danger. The crevices are about fifteen meters (about fifty feet) deep, and deep underground sea water runs into them. Marine life is virtually absent from them, save for a local species of shrimp.

After this little side-trip, continuing along the green track in a southeasterly direction, one comes up with the Mangrove Canal, which runs northwest and southeast, separating the little

Mangroves Island from the mainland. On the island, one can see a small masonry lighthouse, painted black and white.

After reaching the tip of the rocky spit of land, the track turns due north, and returns to the intersection B, by following the west coast of the Hidden Bay. Close to that same curve, just a few feet away from the track, there is a brass plaque set on a cement base which indicates the southernmost tip of the Sinai peninsula (latitude 27° 43' north and longitude 34° 15' east).

One kilometer, or about two-thirds of a mile past the intersection B, one returns to the intersection A, from which one sets out on the second itinerary, marked by the colors purple, red, blue, yellow, and black.

49 center
The coastline immediately adjacent to the Shark Observatory presents rich coral formations. From this point, a foot path allows one to reach the summit of the promontory of Ras Mohammed, where the platform of the Observatory is found.

49 bottom
The Channel of the Mangroves is one of the most distinctive places in the park of Ras Mohammed.

The second route is more complex than the previous one, and it requires several hours. At a distance of two hundred meters (about six hundred fifty feet) past intersection A, on the left of the main track a short track sets off to an elevated observation point; the track is marked by a symbol of a telescope. After passing this track, one reaches intersection C (nine hundred meters, or three thousand feet past intersection A). The track on the right is marked by red and purple arrows, while the left one is marked by red, blue, yellow, black arrows.

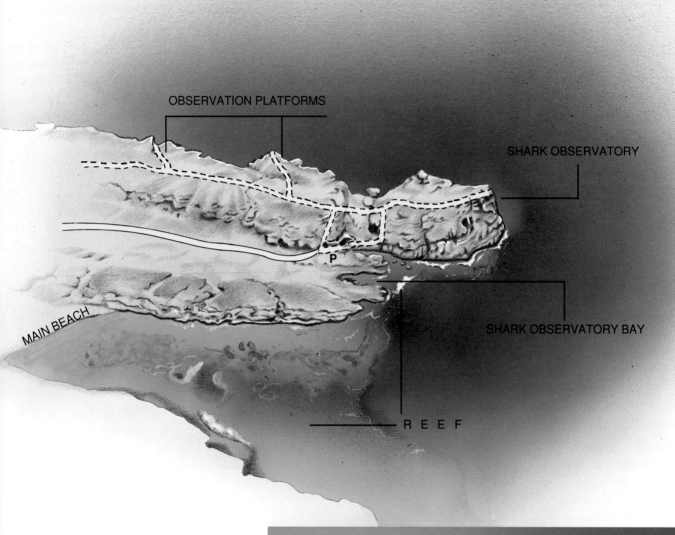

OBSERVATION PLATFORMS

SHARK OBSERVATORY

MAIN BEACH

P

SHARK OBSERVATORY BAY

R E E F

50 The rock that makes up the peninsula of Ras Mohammed is riven in many points by sharp fissures, probably caused by seismic phenomena; the bottom of these crevices is filled with sea water, but the only trace of life is a special local species of shrimp.

Route 2a (red and purple tracks)
Take the right-hand track, which runs along a small extremely saline lake, in which only one form of life survives, a blackish type of algae; after 1.9 kilometers, or just over a mile, one reaches an inlet of Hidden Bay, where a footpath starts toward Yolanda Bay. At a distance of seven hundred meters, or about 2,300 feet past that inlet, one reaches another fork in the road (intersection D): the right-hand track is marked by a red arrow, while the left-hand track is marked by blue, yellow, and black arrows. The right-hand track (red arrow) leads to Yolanda Bay, at a distance of about three-and-a-half kilometers (about two miles).Yolanda Bay received its name because a South African ship named the Yolanda, loaded with ceramic bathroom furnishings sank in the waters off the inlet; the wreck disappeared into the depths after a storm in 1986. From Yolanda Bay a footpath sets out toward the Main Beach.

Route 2b (red, blue, yellow, and black tracks).
At intersection D, one takes the left-hand track (red, blue, yellow, and black arrows) and after one hundred meters (about three hundred thirty feet) one reaches yet another fork in the road (intersection E).
The blue arrow on the right indicates the route toward the Main Beach, at a distance of about six hundred meters (or about two thousand feet); this is a splendid sand beach where one can swim and which is a starting point for a number of dives and underwater itineraries. The arrows on the left, and yellow black in color, indicate routes leading, respectively, to the Shark Observatory Bay (at a distance of

about seven hundred meters, or about 2,300 feet) and to the beaches and underwater sites on the Aqaba side.
The yellow route leads to the Shark Observatory Bay: from here a footpath leads off to the left and up the promontory and reaches the Shark Observatory, a magnificent balcony jutting out fifty-five meters, or about 180 feet, above sea level; from here it is possible to admire the surrounding coral formations and a splendid panorama of the park. After returning to intersection E, and making a right turn here, one follows the route marked by a

black arrow; this route leads to the underwater site of Eel Garden. From here, a footpath leads to two observation platforms. Continuing instead along the main blue track and heading north, one sees, on the right, a second black track which leads to Aqaba Beach, some hundred meters, or three hundred thirty feet, away.
After returning to the blue track, indicated by an exit sign, one heads west and returns to one's starting point (intersection C), at 1.8 kilometers, or just over a mile, from the parking area at intersection E.

51 top
The Channel of the Mangroves, which separates the nearby island from the promontory of Ras Mohammed, takes its name from the numerous mangrove trees (Avicenia marina) that line its banks.

51 center
The shallow blue waters of the Hidden Bay are often populated with waterbirds in search of food.

51 bottom *In the bay of Mersa Bareka, a scientific center is under construction, equipped with laboratories and accommodations for the researchers.*

Underwater itineraries

There are a great many sites along the coasts of Ras Mohammed where it is possible to make some spectacular dives; these sites can be split into two groups, situated respectively on the east and on the west sides of the peninsula.

A Western sites

1) Wreck of the *Thistlegorm*
This may be the finest dive into a wreck in the entire Red Sea. The wreck of the English freighter *Thistlegorm*, bombarded by the Germans in 1941, lies on a sandy floor some thirty meters, or a hundred feet, in depth in the southern section of the reef of Shaab Ali in the Gulf of Suez, to be precise, to the northeast of the site known as Shag Rock. The wreck was discovered in 1956 by commander Cousteau; in order to explore it, one must count on spending two days at sea, because of its distance from Sharm el-Sheikh.

2) Beacon Rock - *Dunraven*
This site is the furthest out, and it is located on the boundaries of the marine area of the Park, at about thirteen kilometers, or eight miles

to the west of Ras Mohammed, about eight kilometers, or five miles, from the coast. At depths ranging from eighteen to twenty-eight meters (sixty to ninety feet), nestled near the coral reef, lies the wreck of the ship *Dunraven*, which sank in 1876 during a voyage from Bombay to Newcastle. There is a chance of encountering sharks here.

3) Small Crack
A channel runs through a sandy lagoon with a great many gorgonians.

4) The Mushroom
A large coral pinnacle rises from the seabed; nearby a shipwreck can be seen at a depth of about twenty meters, or about sixty-five feet.

52 right top
The underwater site known by the name of Alternative Reef, on the west coast of the peninsula of Ras Mohammed is distinguished by extensive coral reefs. Seen from above, the surface of the sea is colored by the delicate hues created by different depths of reef.

52 right center
A cloud of sweepers (Pempheris vanicolensis) flees en masse, frightened by the intrusion of a scuba diver.

52 left center
A solid wall of jacks (Caranx sexfasciatus) swims forward through the deep blue water, scattering silvery reflections.

52 left bottom
Delicately hued alcyonarians, manicolored sponges, and tiny fish incessantly in motion are constants of a great portion of the floor of the Red Sea.

5) Alternative Reef

Around this vast area, which can also be reached by land and which is distinguished by a great many coral reefs. It is possible to make some interesting dives and admire a great abundance of coral reef fish.

6) The Quay (also known as Socony-Vacuum Quay)

Just like at the site mentioned above, it is possible here to dive starting from the coast.
The fauna is a mix of pelagic and reef fish.

53 top right
The Thistlegorm, an armed English freighter, was sunk on 6 October 1941, following a German bombing raid. It was carrying war materiel, twenty trucks, motorcyles, two tanks, two locomotives, and military uniforms. The wreck now lies on a sedimentary seabed some twenty-eight meters (ninety-two feet) beneath the surface.

53 center left
The powerful currents and the abundance of plankton together create the giant sea fans, which are found in many stretches of reefs in the Red Sea.

53 center right
Elegant and many-colored branches of alcyonarians adorn the reef walls, a distinctive and unmistakable adornmento of the Red Sea seabeds.

53 bottom left
Parrotfish (Scaridae) *are marked by their bright coloring and their distinctive beaks, which consist of two powerful dental plates, which allow them to break off and crush the large pieces of coral on which they feed.*

53 bottom righ
Large formations of alcyonarians give the coral reef the appearance of a lush flowering gardens.

B *Eastern sites*

1) Anemone City

Across from Shark Reef, there is an interesting coral reef, which can be reached at about twenty meters, or sixty-five feet, from the shore; at first this formation descends gradually underwater and then suddenly it drops away with a wall from which huge corals extend, waving with the currents; these corals are *Dendronephtya sp.* This site owes its name to the great and remarkable abundance of sea anemones of the species *Radianthus sp.*; there are plenty of gorgonians as well. Typical reef fish are also found in considerable numbers.

2) Shark Reef and Yolanda Reef

Two coral emerging reefs - which rise from a sandy seabed some twenty to thirty meters deep, or between about sixty-five and a hundred feet deep - are the most distinctive features of this splendid diving site, set a few hundred meters (yards) from the coast, right in line with the easternmost tip of the Hidden Bay, where it is possible to admire a great many species of pelagic fish.
This is one of the most heavily visited sites, but the presence of powerful currents makes it inadvisable for beginners.
There is a chance of encountering sharks here.

3) Shark Observatory

Directly beneath the observation platform known as Shark Observatory, and accessible by following one of the overland routes, one can admire a magnificent coral reef that plunges down to depths of up to ninety meters (about three hundred feet), with a great many species of pelagic fish. There is a chance of encountering sharks.

4) Eel Garden

In this site, which can also be reached by land (see Route 2b), it is possible to see a great number of eels (*Gorgasia sillneri*) on a sandy seabed, some ten to fifteen meters (thirty-five to fifty feet) deep

54 top One of the most renowned underwater sites at Ras Mohammed is the Shark Reef, made up of two coral banks that break the surface in the southeaster corner of Hidden Bay.

54 bottom A veritable wall of batfish (Platax orbicularis) moves implacably before the camera lens and photographer.

5) Ras Atar

At Ras Atar, which marks one end of the deep bay of Marsa Bareka, a reef drops down to a depth of about forty-five meters (about a hundred fifty feet), with an abundance of pelagic fish and gorgonians.

6) Marsa Bareka

In this great bay with its sandy seabeds, and an average depth of twenty-five meters (eighty feet), one can tour a large grotto. This dive can only be made from a boat.

7) Ras Ghazlani

This site is in a line with the eastern cape of the bay (on the side opposite Ras Atar) and is remarkable for its abundance of pelagic fish and for its imposing of coral formations.

55 top left
*A splendid specimen of the turkeyfish (*Pterois volitans*) perches upon a branch of gorgonian.*

55 bottom left
*A humphead wrasse (*Cheilinus undulatus*) patrols the alcyonarian-decked walls of the reef.*

55 top right
*A coral grouper (*Cephalopholis miniata*) peers out of his den amongst corals and alcyonarians.*

55 center right
Enormous formations of gorgonians grow along the reef walls, extending out toward the open water.

55 bottom right
*Recognizable by its distinctively shaped head, a hammerhead shark (*Sphyrna lewini*) swims powerfully and majestically through the depths.*

PRACTICAL INFORMATION

The Park is open from dawn to dusk, and the cost of admission is five dollars US per person; an entrance fee of five dollars US must also be paid for automobiles.

At the ticket booth, one can also obtain a little leaflet about the Park, containing all sorts of information and regulations governing the protected areas. It is possible to camp only in the designated areas - generally well-protected little bays - near the Operations Center of the park personnel, and one must ask for prior authorization at the ticket booth or in the Park offices.

At the Visitors' Center is a coffee shop, open from 8 am to 6 pm. In the same complex as the cafeteria, there should soon be a number of souvenir shops, a bookstore, and a library.

In order to travel from Sharm el-Sheikh to Ras Mohammed, one must show one's passport at the Egyptian army checkpoint.

56 top In this remarkable photograph, we see the savage beauty of the coasts of the Sinai and the remarkable wealth of the beds of the Red Sea.

56 bottom Turkeyfish (Pterois volitans) are equipped with venomous spines that can inflict painful stings which can in turn provoke dangerous fevers.

57 top left
The streamlined body of a number of great barracudas (Sphyraena qenie) *scatter silvery highlights across the seabeds.*

57 top right
Along the reef walls, the alcyonarians are certainly the most impressive piece of underwater stagecraft.

57 center right
A group of masked butterflyfish (Chaetodon semilarvatus) *swims just off the reef.*

57 bottom left
A voracious predator, the coral grouper (Cephalopholis miniata) *feeds on the smaller fish that live along the walls of the coral reef.*

58 top The long tentacles of a sea anemone offer refuge and protection to a pair of clownfish (Amphiprion bicinctus).

58 center A school of glassfish (Parapriachantus guentheri) passed in procession before the entrance of an underwater grotto.

58 bottom The flashlight of a scuba diver brightens the colors of the alcyonarians and emphasizes the delicate structure of the branches of the gorgonians.

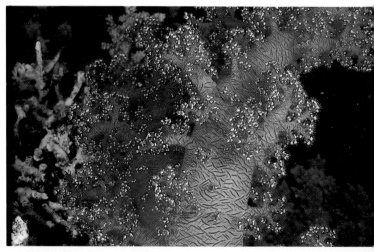

59 top left
Long considered —
mistakenly — to be
forms of plant life,
alcyonarians
actually belong to
the class of the
octocorallia, since
they are formed of
micropolyps with
eight tentacles.

59 top right
A splendid pink
alcyonarian, swollen
with water and with
the tentacles of its
polyps extended, is
probably filter-
feeding on the
plankton floating in
suspension in the
underwater currents.

59 center right
Great gorgonian
fans always
develop parallel to
the flow of the main
currents, which
channel the
microrganisms on
which the coral
polyps feed.

59 bottom left
Rather timid and
recalcitrant, the
larger snappers
(Lutjanus bohar)
tend to shy away
from the reefs
where most of the
new tourism
concentrates.

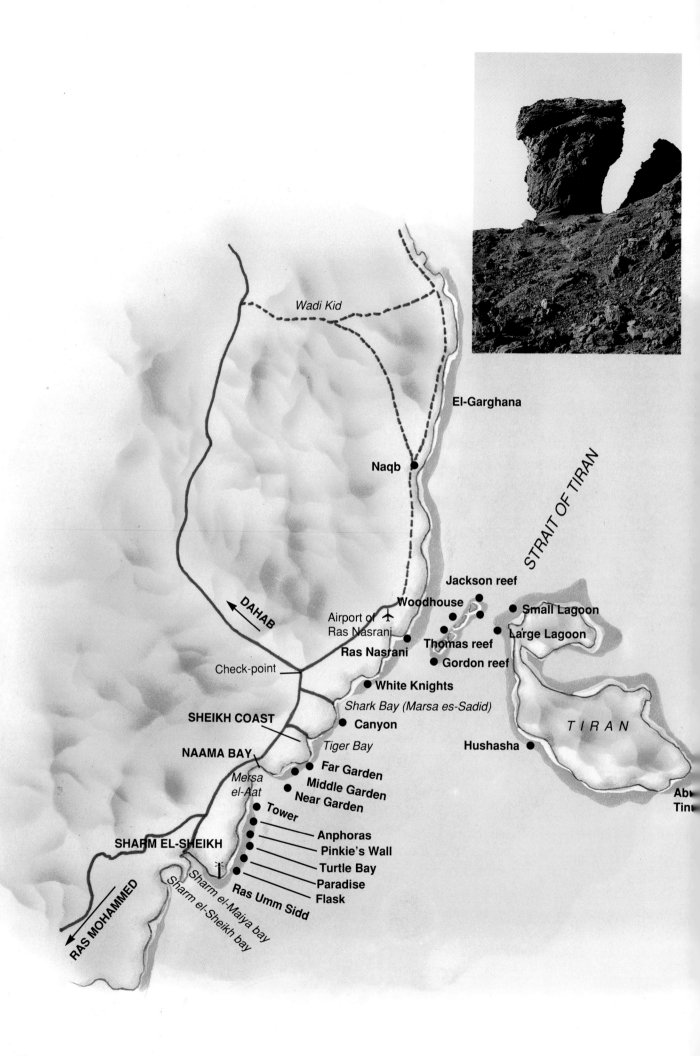

Wadi Kid

El-Garghana

Naqb

STRAIT OF TIRAN

DAHAB

Jackson reef

Woodhouse

Small Lagoon

Airport of
Ras Nasrani

Thomas reef

Large Lagoon

Ras Nasrani

Gordon reef

Check-point

White Knights

TIRAN

SHEIKH COAST

Shark Bay (Marsa es-Sadid)

Canyon

NAAMA BAY

Tiger Bay

Hushasha

Mersa
el-Aat

Far Garden

Middle Garden

Near Garden

Tower

SHARM EL-SHEIKH

Anphoras

Pinkie's Wall

Turtle Bay

RAS MOHAMMED

Ras Umm Sidd

Paradise

Flask

Sharm el-Maiya bay

Sharm el-Sheikh bay

Abu
Tin

60

SHARM EL-SHEIKH

Sharm el-Sheikh is a small town built in 1968 and located on the eastern shore of the deep inlet of Sharm el-Maiya, upon a rocky spit that extends southward the promontory of Ras Umm Sidd. The bay of Sharm el-Maiya contains a small marina for pleasure craft; it is surrounded by hotels and shops, while further to the west, separated from the bay of Sharm el-Maiya, opens out the bay of Sharm el-Sheikh.

In this bay there is a harbor under military surveillance; this is the home port to a number of coast guard vessels, some of them belonging to Egypt, others belonging to the Italian navy and forming part of the multinational armed forces. In this second bay, the boat that links Sharm el-Sheikh with Hurgada every day arrives on a daily basis. From Sharm el-Sheikh the road continues northward until it reaches the ample inlet of Naama Bay, at a distance of seven kilometers (about four-and-a-half miles). At about two kilometers, or about a mile, from the edge of the town of Sharm, one may notice an odd limestone boulder on the left which has been shaped by the weather and the elements and today bears a striking resemblance to the profile of John F. Kennedy. At Naama Bay, in the space of a very few years, the true center of tourism in the southern Sinai has sprung up; most of the hotels and diving centers are here. After passing by Naama Bay, the road continues along, parallel with the coast, where there are three other inlets less impressive in size. The second of these inlets, now known as Coral Bay, is the site of the largest residential tourist resort in the entire Sinai peninsula; it is known as Sheikh Coast. The third inlet, called Shark Bay, possesses a series of bungalows, with an adjacent restaurant and a diving center, both of which can be reached by following the tracks, which split off from the main road, at distances of - respectively - three and six kilometers (two and four

miles) from Naama. The road continues in a northerly direction until Ras Nasrani, where the international airport is located; here, after a checkpoint manned by the Egyptian army, the road heads northwest, linking Sharm el-Sheikh to Dahab. If one sets out from Sharm el-Sheikh, or better yet, from Naama Bay, it is possible to make a series of excursions out into the surrounding desert, or to make dives to the seabeds off the coast between the bay of Sharm el-Maiya and Ras Nasrani.

60 This huge limestone boulder, located at the outskirts of Sharm el-Sheikh along the road that leads to Naama Bay, is one of the great oddities of Sharm: the profile shape by the elements into the rock is reminiscent of the silhouette of the late American president, John F. Kennedy.

SANAFIR

61 top The island of Tiran, along with the smaller island of Sanafir, seals off the Gulf of Eilat to the south, forming the strait of Tiran. These islands, which

belong to Saudi Arabia but given to Egypt for its use, form part of a protected area that has been annexed to the the National Park of Ras Mohammed.

61 bottom The bay of Sharm el-Maiya is bounded to the east by the promontory of Ras Um Sidd, and to the west by a spit of land that separates it from a second bay called Sharm el-Sheikh.

62 top The village of Sharm el-Sheikh was built around Sharm el-Maiya, has become one of the most popular destinations for vacationing European scuba divers.

62 center Aerial view of the eastern side of the bay of Sharm el-Maiya, with the lovely beach and the huge hotel complex of the Hilton Residence.

62 bottom and 63 top Sharm el-Maiya possesses the most popular marina for tourism in all of the southern Sinai, and the numbers of pleasure boats that anchor grows constantly.

63 bottom The coastline to the west of the lighthouse of Ras Umm Sidd is marked by the extensive coral reef and a very high cliff.

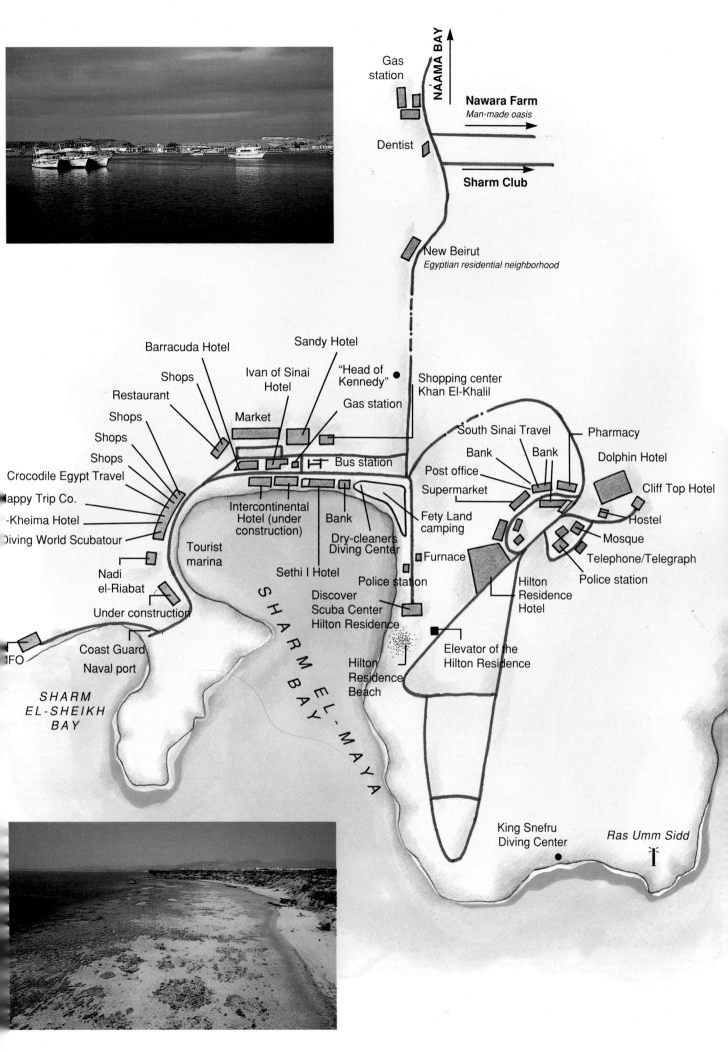

NAAMA BAY

Gas station

Nawara Farm
Man-made oasis

Dentist

Sharm Club

New Beirut
Egyptian residential neighborhood

Barracuda Hotel

Sandy Hotel

Shops

Ivan of Sinai Hotel

"Head of Kennedy"

Shopping center Khan El-Khalil

Restaurant

Shops

Market

Gas station

South Sinai Travel

Pharmacy

Shops

Bank

Bank

Dolphin Hotel

Shops

Bus station

Post office

Cliff Top Hotel

Crocodile Egypt Travel

Supermarket

Happy Trip Co.

Intercontinental Hotel (under construction)

Bank

Fety Land camping

Hostel

-Kheima Hotel

Dry-cleaners Diving Center

Mosque

Diving World Scubatour

Furnace

Telephone/Telegraph

Tourist marina

Sethi I Hotel

Police station

Police station

Nadi el-Riabat

Discover Scuba Center Hilton Residence

Hilton Residence Hotel

Under construction

Coast Guard

Elevator of the Hilton Residence

IFO

Naval port

Hilton Residence Beach

SHARM EL-SHEIKH BAY

SHARM EL-MAYA

King Snefru Diving Center

Ras Umm Sidd

63

NAAMA BAY

65 top left
The landing dock,
located at the
southernmost tip of
Naama Bay, is a
rendez-vous point
for the scuba divers
who set out each
morning to dive in
many different sites.

65 bottom left
The beach of Naama
Bay is equipped
with a considerable
array of tourist
facilities, allowing
one to select among
many different sorts
of water sports.

65 right
Naama Bay,
situated just a few
kilometers north of
Sharm el-Sheikh,
has in the past few
years developed
into the leading
tourist attraction of
the entire Sinai, and
it has witnessed a
real boom in the
construction of
hotels.

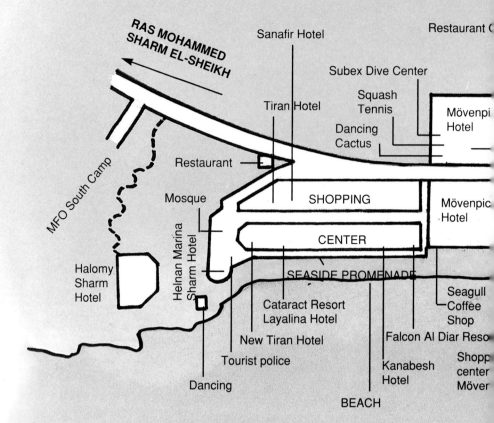

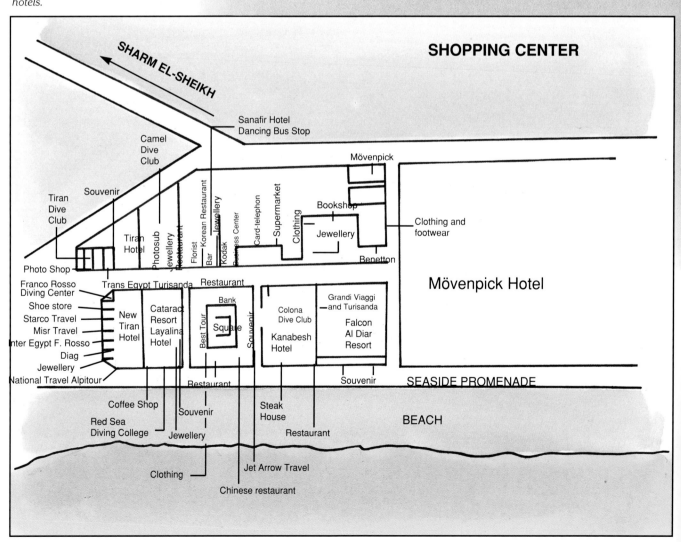

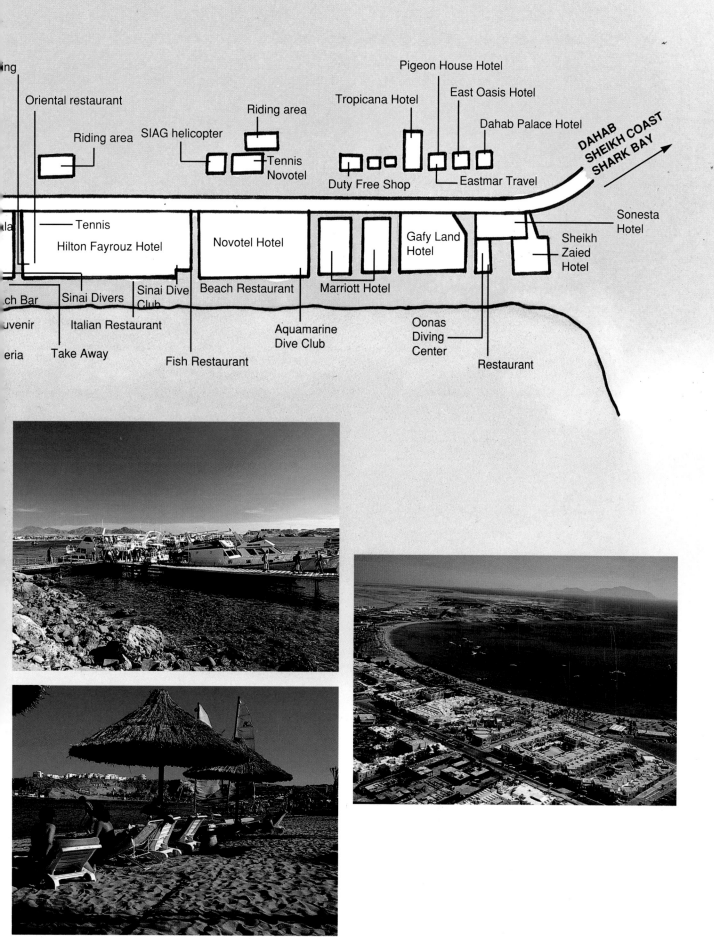

Oriental restaurant

Riding area

SIAG helicopter

Riding area

Tropicana Hotel

Pigeon House Hotel

East Oasis Hotel

Dahab Palace Hotel

DAHAB
SHEIKH COAST
SHARK BAY

Tennis
Novotel

Duty Free Shop

Eastmar Travel

Tennis

Hilton Fayrouz Hotel

Novotel Hotel

Gafy Land
Hotel

Sonesta
Hotel

Sheikh
Zaied
Hotel

ch Bar

Sinai Divers

Sinai Dive
Club

Beach Restaurant

Marriott Hotel

uvenir

Italian Restaurant

Aquamarine
Dive Club

Oonas
Diving
Center

eria

Take Away

Fish Restaurant

Restaurant

65

66 top The coasts of Naama Bay, despite the high concentration of tourist structures, still maintain a number of points that are pristine, especially in the northern section, where there are a number of coral reefs, such as the Near Garden and the Far Garden, destination for many scuba divers.

66 center The new residential complex of Sheikh Coast spreads on the shores of a large bay to the north of Naama Bay.

66 bottom At Shark Bay, immediately to the north of Sheikh Coast, there is a tourist village and a well-equipped diving center.

67 top
The numerous tourist resorts and diving centers that have sprung up over the past few years ensure a perfect accommodation for those who love the sea and who love to dive.

67 center
The warm colors of the Sinai desert contrast with the deep blue of the waters of the Red Sea.

67 bottom
The lighthouse, immediately to the north of Ras Nasrani, warns ships of the entrance to the Strait of Tiran and was built on a stretch of coral reef that separates the deep waters of the Gulf of Eilat from a shallow inland lagoon.

Underwater Itineraries

There are a great many interesting diving sites along the coast between Sharm el-Sheikh and Ras Nasrani. Among the most important, let us mention:

1) The Temple
This is a diving site used by many diving centers for the first, orientation dives, and it takes its name from the three large pinnacles that rise from the seabed like the columns of a temple.

2) Ras Umm Sid
Not far from the lighthouse of Ras Umm Sidd, close to the previous site, it is possible admire a full-fledged underwater forest of gorgonians, amidst glassfish and small *Anthias.*

3) Amphoras
This site takes its name from the presence of the wreck a sixteenth-century ship that was transporting amphoras full of mercury.

4) Tower
This is a steep underwater scarp that drops down to a depth of about sixty meters, or 197 feet.

5) Near Garden
Situated on the northern side of Naama Bay, this site allows one to make dives no deeper than thirty meters, or a hundred feet.

6) Far Garden
Situated just to the north of Near Garden, Far Garden allows divers to admire underwater grottoes that open in the wall at a depth of about ten meters, or just over thirty feet.

7) Shark Bay
The dive takes place on a coral reef that lies in the southern part of the bay, and is crossed by a small canyon.

68 top and center
The promontory of Ras Umm Sid, with its lighthouse, marks the easternmost limitation of the bay of Sharm el-Maiya. The remarkable development of the coral reef makes this stretch of sea one of the most popular destinations of scuba divers.

68 bottom
The coastline to the north of Sharm el-Sheikh, in line with the site of Nabq, is lined by a major coral reef and by a large forest of mangroves.

8) Ras Nasrani

In a line with the huge coral reef that runs around the promontory of Ras Nasrani, it is possible to dive to a depth of some twenty meters (sixty-five feet) and admire abundant reef fauna. Another dive can be done just north of there, across from the lighthouse of Ras Nasrani, where the coral reef drops down to a depth of some forty-five meters (one hundred forty-five feet).

9) Strait of Tiran

As of this writing, one can dive over the Gordon and the Jackson reefs. In both sites, the coral reefs drops down to a depth of some seventy meters (two hundred thirty feet). It is also possible to observe a handsome array of deep-sea fauna (sharks have been observed there); the currents are quite powerful.

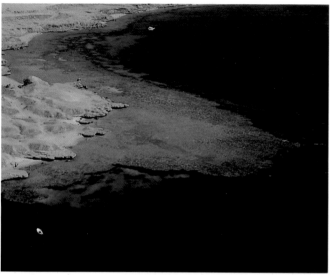

69 top left This aerial photograph allows us to see clearly the point where the coral reef plunges down into the depths of the sea. In this photograph, we can see Near Garden, one of the most popular sites for diving, not far from Naama.

69 center left A grouper (Plectropomus marisrubri) seeks refuge beneath a jutting section of reef, amidst the inevitable multicolored alcyonarians.

69 center right The remarkable size to which alcyonarians grow in the Red Sea is a result of the fact that the water temperature never drops below 20° Centigrade.

69 bottom left Banner butterflyfish (Heniochus diphreutes) are marked by the two broad dark stripes that run across their disk-shaped bodies and by their exceedingly long caudal fin.

70 top A large umbrella formation of acropora, which looms over a number of remarkable formations of brain coral, offers shelter and protection to the smaller reef fish.

70 center The dark waters of the night serve to highlight the delicate structure of these sea fans, which form a veritable undersea forest.

70 bottom At just a few centimeters from the surface, the reef shows forth its inexhaustible wealth, allowing even those who are not scuba divers to glimpse the undersea fauna and flora.

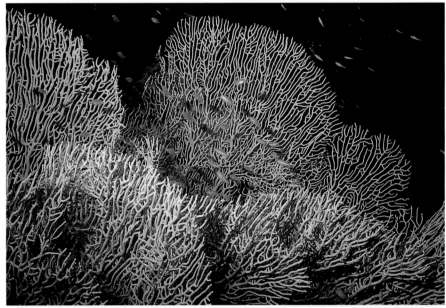

71 top left
Branches of gorgonians, sponges, and coral entirely cover the walls of an undersea grotto, creating a remarkable scene.

71 bottom left
A turkeyfish (Pterois volitans) shows off its pectoral fins, which a diaphanous membrane renders similar to feathers.

71 top right
This macro photograph allows us to observe in considerable detail the tiny polyps gaping open on a branch of alcyonarian, as well as the transparent structure of the cenosarco, which constitutes the epidermis of the colony.

71 bottom right
A small but daring clownfish (Amphiprion bicinctus) ventures out of the safety of the tentacles of the sea anemone, to swim threateningly toward the scuba diver that has invaded his territory.

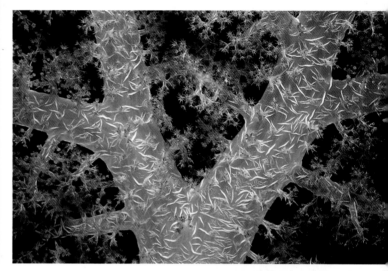

Land routes

WADI EL-AAT

The true Beduin name of Naama Bay is Marsa el-Aat, meaning the Bay of el-Aat. In this area, the broad bed of the Wadi el-Aat ends its run to the sea.

Many hotels and the shopping center of Sharm Mall have been built at the mouth of the wadi, without the slightest consideration for the danger in case of flooding. In order to diminish the danger, to the north of the Hotel Mövenpick, a dam has been built which seals off the Wadi el-Aat, blocking its rushing waters. This dam can be seen from the new asphalt road, still under construction as of this writing, built in order to reroute heavy truck traffic away from the residential center.

Itinerary

If one is coming from Naama Bay, one takes a right turn immediately after the Mobil gas station.

After about two kilometers, or just over a mile, the road becomes a track and divides at a fork. Take the right-hand track and a little later the road will intersect with the new ring road, and then pass it by. Also on the right one passes a Beduin village made up of sheds made of sheet metal and rocks. Immediately after that village, on the right, tower the three granitic peaks of the Gebel Ruwesat el-Nima, from which it is possible to enjoy a fine view of the Wadi el-Aat Sharqui; one can get a glimpse of the dam here. The clear and well made track curves around this isolated mountain and heads north, skirting the Gebel Dagilat. At a distance of about eight-and-a-half kilometers (about five miles) from the beginning of the track one comes to another fork in the track: the track leading off to the left heads west, to a granite quarry, where one can see enormous blocks of stone being split with a technique not unlike that used in the time of the pharaohs. At this point, one should avoid driving onto a track that cuts off toward the left. Instead, continue along the track on the right, which runs along the bed of the Wadi el-Aat,

leaving Gebel Wair on the right. The track then comes to another Beduin village, splitting the settlement in two. It would be best to drive around the village, making a wide left-hand loop, lest one disturb the villagers in their daily activities. There are a number of interesting ancient stone constructions built against huge granite boulders. After passing the village, the track continues, drifting slightly to the left, entering the northernmost section of the Wadi el-Aat and skirting the magnificent reddish basalt ridges that break the monotony of the granite boulders. The track continues, intersected by the ruts of the many jeeps that cut off in search of easier routes. Continuing in the same direction, one arrives after seven-and-a-half kilometers (about five miles) at a handsome ravine cut into the grey granite, where large pink granite boulders are scattered and dikes of basalt; this is "Aed el-Aat," the reservoir for the water of Wadi el-Aat. In fact, in the winter, after a bit of rain, small waterfalls form, filling

every recess with water; animals come to drink thirstily. Even in the dry season, however, it is sufficient to dig into the rough sand and one will find enough water to slake the thirst of camels. After leaving the automobile, one can take a brief stroll amongst the enormous boulders lodged against the walls of the canyon. After a short distance, on the left, one can see a camel path: the Beduins in fact use a trail that links Wadi el-Aat directly with the slope of el-Tor.

Even in the middle of the summer, this place maintains a bit of coolness, in the shade of huge rock boulders and many acacia trees. Along the return route, when one reaches the intersection that stands at a distance of about eight-and-a-half kilometers (about five miles) from the beginning of the track, one can take any of the numerous trails heading in an easterly direction, and - after crossing a vast uphill stretch of granitic sand - reach Naama Bay. One continues

(Map labels, right margin:) Gebel Aat el-Sharqi — Aed — Gebel Aat el-Garib — Gebel Madsus

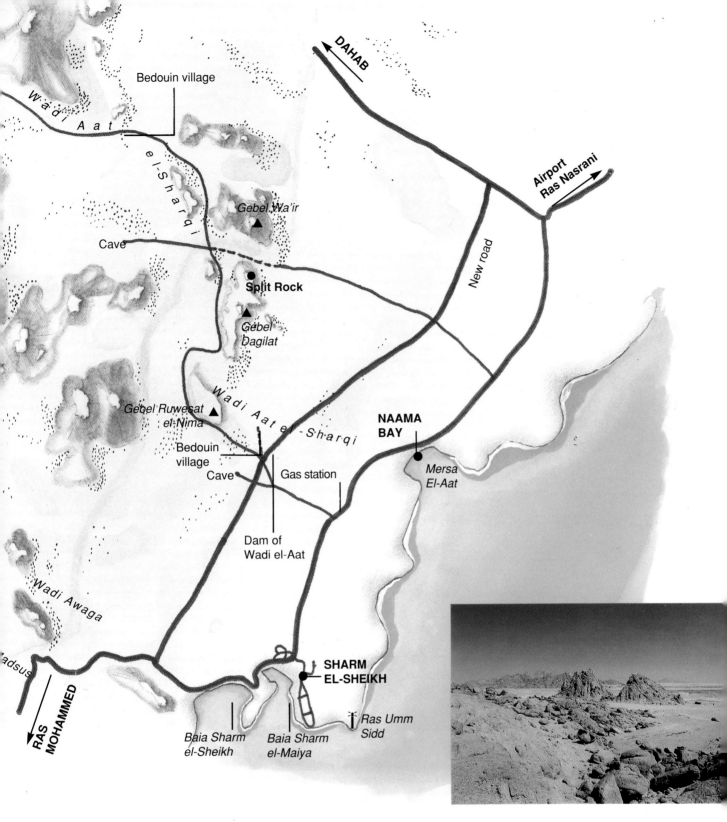

Map labels:

DAHAB

Airport
Ras Nasrani

Wadi Aat

Bedouin village

el-Sharqi

Gebel Wa'ir

Cave

Split Rock

Gebel Dagilat

New road

Gebel Ruwesat el-Nima

Wadi Aat el-Sharqi

NAAMA BAY

Bedouin village

Cave

Gas station

Dam of Wadi el-Aat

Mersa El-Aat

Wadi Awaga

adsus

RAS MOHAMMED

SHARM EL-SHEIKH

Baia Sharm el-Sheikh

Baia Sharm el-Maiya

Ras Umm Sidd

along straight, and one will easily mistake the desert horizon for glimpses of the sea in the distance. On the right, one will note "Split Rock," a huge split boulder, a meeting spot for the residents of Sharm el-Sheikh who use this as a starting point for night-time festivals in the desert. At a distance of about six kilometers (about four miles) from "Split Rock," there is a new, asphalt, ring road that skirts Naama Bay and runs parallel with the coast. Cross this road and continue along straight and one will reach the main road linking Naama Bay with Sheikh Coast.

This excursion is neither long nor particularly challenging, but often the tracks are muddled and difficult to follow, or else erased or altered by the rains. Therefore, we would advise anyone who does not know the area or who is not experienced in desert travel to contact a Beduin guide who can lead the party, or, at the very least, to advise the authorities before setting out.

72 The deepest and most entrancing part of the Wadi el-Aat is constituted by a narrow canyon which can be entered only on foot or by camel.

73 The granite peaks of the Gebel Ruwesat el-Nima, which can be seen as one climbs the Wadi al-Aat, stand a few kilometers, or miles, from the coast.

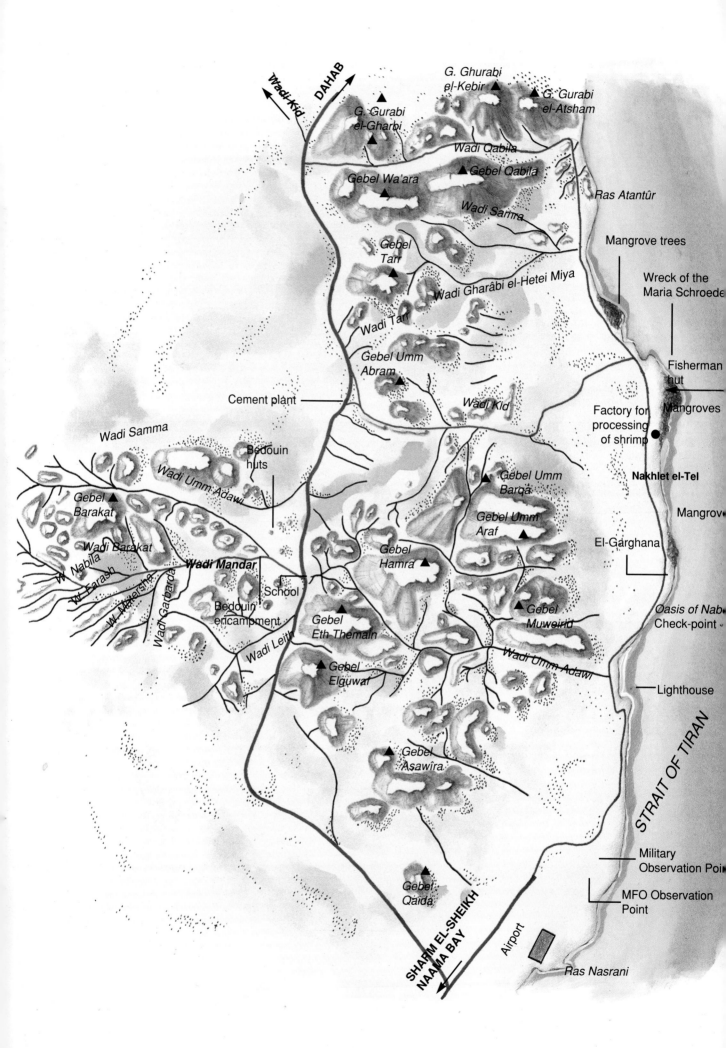

Wadi-Kid

DAHAB

G. Ghurabi
el-Kebir

G. Gurabi
el-Atsham

G. Gurabi
el-Gharbi

Wadi Qabila

Gebel Qabila

Gebel Wa'ara

Ras Atantûr

Wadi Samra

Mangrove trees

Gebel
Tarr

Wreck of the
Maria Schroeder

Wadi Gharâbi el-Hetei Miya

Wadi Tarr

Gebel Umm
Abram

Fisherman
hut

Wâdi Kid

Mangroves

Cement plant

Factory for
processing
of shrimp

Wadi Samma

Nakhlet el-Tel

Bedouin
huts

Gebel Umm
Barqa

Wadi Umm Adawi

Gebel
Barakat

Gebel Umm
Araf

Mangrove

Wadi Barakat

Gebel
Hamra

El-Garghana

W. Nabila

W. Farash

Wadi Mandar

School

Gebel
Muweirid

Oasis of Nab
Check-point

Bedouin
encampment

W. Makersha

Wâdi Garbarda

Wadi Leith

Gebel
Eth Themain

Wadi Umm Adawi

Lighthouse

Gebel
Elguwat

STRAIT OF TIRAN

Gebel
Asawîra

Military
Observation Poi

MFO Observation
Point

Gebel
Qaida

SHARM EL-SHEIKH
NAAMA BAY

Airport

Ras Nasrani

WADI MANDAR

This is a brief and not very demanding excursion, in the soft light of afternoon, when the colors and shapes of the rocks stand out and are outlined at their sharpest. It is at any rate advisable upon one's return to reach the paved road as the light of the day is fading, illuminating the various tracks that intersect on the sand - the dying light is especially helpful in avoiding the deep sand.

Itinerary

If one takes the Sharm-Dahab road, at a distance of 20.3 kilometers (12.5 miles) from the Egyptian army checkpoint, Wadi Mandar opens out to the left of the paved road. It is easy to recognize the entrance, as it is next to a white schoolhouse, at the beginning of the track, where Beduin children attend school. Here, there are numerous sheet-metal shacks belonging to sedentary Beduins, who will be glad to rent their camels to anyone who wishes to leave their car for a while. (Plan on spending 25/30 Egyptian pounds for an hour's ride, with a guide).
Those who decide to continue in their cars must make an attempt to follow the main, well beaten track. The valley is made up of a succession of amble plains dotted with numerous acacia trees, bounded by low granite hills, cut by basalt veins and dikes, which mark a black network in the lighter colored intrusive rocks.
At a distance of thirteen kilometers (about eight miles) from the track, the wadi is sealed off to the right by a high wall of rocks and detritus.

75 An excursion to the Wadi Mandar offers a chance to travel through a remarkable and wild landscape, just a stone's-throw from Naama Bay. Along the walls of the wadi, one can admire a number of magnificent dykes, infiltrations of blackish volcanic rock amidst the preexisting granite formations, which are reddish in color.

WADI KID - OASIS OF AIN KID

Wadi Kid begins its route in the heart of the Central Massif of the Sinai, and then runs into the Gulf of Eilat on a line with Nabq. This excursion primarily involves the part of the wadi that runs in a northwesterly direction, to the left of the paved road.

Itinerary

The track that runs along the wadi and leads to the oasis of Ain Kid begins at a distance of 41.6 kilometers (twenty-six miles) from the Egyptian military checkpoint. There is nothing that clearly indicates the mouth of the wadi. The track, which sinks a couple of meters (yards) beneath the level of the paved road, can be seen very clearly once one is driving along it - there are no stretches of deep sand, and the bed of the track is made up of breccia.

76 top If one continues along the Wadi Kid on foot, one will enter a valley, with a few well watered areas, abounding in palms, with small cultivated gardens and stone houses used by the Beduins.

76 center The Wadi Kid ends in a narrow gorge, where one must park one's four-wheel drive vehicle and continue on foot, passing through an area of jagged surfaces and large boulders.

76 bottom For its great beauty, variety of landscapes, and proximity to Naama Bay, the Wadi Kid is nowadays one of the most popular tourist destinations.

At a distance of 13.5 kilometers (about eight-and-a-half miles) from the entrance to the wadi, there is a formation on the right made up of smooth, rounded pink granite, riven here and there by deep fissures. After one kilometer, also on the right of the track, one encounters the only Beduin village in the valley, inhabited throughout the year, and built upon a terrace of boulders, sheltered from raging floodwaters in case of torrential desert rains. Immediately afterward begin the first walled gardens; one may notice two black plastic pipes that bring water to the village, running on the right at the base of the rocks. At a distance of 16.5 kilometers (about ten miles) from the entrance, an interesting group of granite rocks made up by a base with two huge boulders perched atop it looms at the center of the wadi. In the meanwhile, the rock walls draw ever closer, narrowing the canyon, and closing with slight rightward curve in a lovely interplay of geometric forms. Leave the car here and take the trail on the right to begin an interesting hike: the place is wild and uncultivated, but the presence of an abundant water table permits the survival of acacias, fruit trees, and luxuriant palm trees.

After two or three passages of some slight difficulty, amidst the huge granite boulders, the trail continues without obstacles. The mountains on all sides are tall and austere, and the silence is interrupted only by the singing of a few birds and by the rustling of the wind in the palm fronds.

On the right there is a curious dome-shaped rock, while at the center of the trail, a low wall has been built to serve as a dam to capture rain water. Immediately beyond this wall, one finds a few rock lean-tos scattered here and there beneath the palm trees, inhabited almost exclusively during the season of the date harvest. There are a great many wells, and nearly all of them are built out of rocks. Ain Kid is a full-fledged garden of date palms enclosed on all sides by mountains, and there is still not very much tourism here.

77 top It is very common in the upper stretches of the Wadi Kid to encounter Beduins that live in the area, taking advantage of its relative abundance of water, which permits them to eke out a little farming.

77 center and below The eastern section of the Wadi Kid consists of limestone and sandstone formations which often display very visible signs of the erosion practiced by the wind and weather on these soft rock formations dating from the Tertiary Period.

NATIONAL PARK OF NABQ - OASIS OF MANGROVES - WADI QABILA

The route to cover runs from the so-called eastern track, a white road that is largely well beaten, used by Beduin fishermen, and only recently discovered by tourists.

The region of Nabq, which extends over six hundred square kilometers (two hundred square miles), was declared to be protected territory and incorporated in 1992 into the National Park of Ras Mohammed. The delicate natural equilibrium of this coastal strip justifies the policy of extremely strict environmental protection that is implemented by the Park authorities. These places of great beauty offer the visitor an opportunity to observe a lagoon area, teeming with life, in contrast with the silent void of the surrounding desert. The hermit and mud crabs are among the most numerous inhabitants of these beachs, and the mud crabs in particular play a role of great importance thanks to their frenetic digging, which contibutes to a continual blending of sediments, with consequential oxygenation and fertilization of the earth. At Nabq one can see the largest mangrove forest in all of the Sinai, which extends along more than four kilometers (two-and-a-half miles) of the shoreline. These plants, with their distinctive roots on the water's surface and the lower face of their leaves rough with salt, belong to the species of *Avicenia marina*, a special type of mangrove common to this area, whose roots are able to filter sea water and expel salt crystals from the leaves. Mangroves, moreover, are

78 top
Aerial view of the impressive coral formations that stretch from Ras Nasrani to the oasis of Nabq. The beach shown is fringed by dense stands of mangroves.

78 bottom
The "mangrove forest," located in the protected area of Nabq, to the north of Naama Bay, is the largest and most important one in the Sinai. Mangroves (Avicenia marina) filter seawater, expelling salt crystals from their leaves.

important because their roots manage to restrain sediments, thus limiting the erosion of the entire coast line. The oasis of mangroves in the Park of Nabq is considered the northernmost point in the entire Red Sea-Indian Ocean complex in which *Avicenia marina* has developed. Nabq is home to a vast number of animal genera and species, which can be observed here - from the smallest fishes that come here to deposit their eggs in the shallow, safe waters that surround the mangroves, to the numerous

different birds that nest in their branches, near the sea where food is available in great abundance. In the oasis of Nabq, it is common to observe white herons and grey herons, see large ospreys and, during the migrating season, storks. The wadis that run all the way to the coast, in this protected area, present a type of vegetation that is unique to the southern Sinai, and which provides an ideal habitat for a number of wild animals (foxes, gazelles, hyenas, and other animals) while also playing a role in regulating the movement of the sand dunes.

79 top Recently the protected area of Nabq was joined with the National Park of Ras Mohammed and subjected to strict protection, required in order to preserve this environment intact.

79 center
Plantlife in the oasis of Nabq is not limited to the mangroves, but also includes many species of palm tree.

79 bottom
Many crustaceans live by digging dens in the very shallow waters that surround the mangroves.

Itinerary
After passing the airport of Ras Nasrani, the paved road runs through the desert, amongst mine fields protected by barbed wire. On the right, there is a military base of the MFO, well positioned overlooking the Strait of Tiran. A few meters (yards) further along, after a small paved area that was built to serve as a heliport, a road starts off on the right and leads to an old military observation point used during the wars between Egypt and Israel. The cement platform, in a bad state of repair, was the foundation for a large piece of heavy artillery used to control the passage through the strait. The road continues, at this point no longer paved, and - after

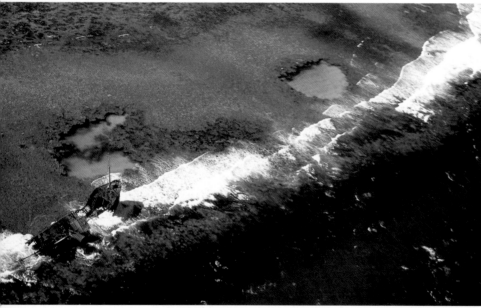

a few curves - heads off on the right, running parallel with the coast. On the horizon, on the far side of the Gulf of Eilat , one can just glimpse Saudi Arabia.

At a distance of six-and-a-half kilometers (four miles) from the old military observation point, the road runs by one of the strait's lighthouses and, a few meters (yards) further along, the road intersects with another track running northeast.

At a distance of 9.7 kilometers (six miles) from the observation point is the small oasis of Nabq. The checkpoint of the Egyptian army is concealed amidst the luxuriant fronds of palm trees, which mark the presence of a fairly important underground water-bearing stratum.

The soldiers here generally check one's passport. At a distance of four kilometers (two-and-a-half miles) from the military checkpoint, one encounters the first group of mangroves, on the site known as Naklet el-Tel (or also el-Garghana). A number of families of Beduin fishermen live year round in the nearby village of a few huts made of sheet metal and palm fronds. The local population tends to increase during the migratory season of the snapper (*Lutjanus bohar*), which the locals call *shaour*, a large silvery fish, which swims in schools from the Gulf of Eilat during the mating season to reach the warmer waters of Ras Mohammed. The track continues along the coast and, after a curve around a handsome thicket of palms, passes near a green sheet-metal construction, with large tanks used in breeding shrimp. This is the first experiment in aquaculture set up in the southern Sinai, under the auspices of the National Park, and it constitutes part of a larger economic development program in the area, designed to provide adequate employment for the Beduins who live there. At a distance of ten kilometers (six-and-a-quarter miles) past the Egyptian checkpoint, the track splits and, on the right, leads on into the heart of a white-sand lagoon with exceedingly warm water (from May to October), surrounded by a dense stand of mangroves which extends along the coral reef for about four kilometers (two-and-a-half miles) of coastline. On the left is the gutted wreck of *Maria Schroeder*, a ship that sank on the coral reefs in 1965, a silent witness to the dangers of these waters for passing ships. On the beach, Bedouin fishermen have built a little base. They gather in the little hut made out of bits of wood and palm fronds in order to untangle their nets, repairing rips with large hooked needles, and to cook their unleavened bread on disks of metal placed directly over the burner, and to drink tea.

A very important activity is the drying of the fish that are cleaned and chopped up, and then sprinkled with sea salt scraped off the rocks during low tide and spread out to dry in the rays of the sun, atop the roof of the hut, for a number of days. After leaving the oasis of mangroves, at a distance of fourteen kilometers (about nine miles) from the army checkpoint, on the right one finds a small cluster of palm trees, enclosed by a low wall. A few meters (yards) further along, on the left, there is an alternative route, marked for Wadi Kid (here it is also called Wadi Khresa). The track for Wadi Kid is broad and very comfortable, and leads directly to the paved road that links Sharm el-Sheikh with Dahab, in line with the cement factory. An alternative and far less developed route is that along the track through the Wadi Khabila. After leaving the mangrove oasis, one continues along the eastern track. After passing a second lagoon, which is smaller but no less enchanting than the oasis, the track continues along the coast. At about nineteen kilometers (about twelve miles) past the check point, just past a small stone building, one turns off on the left into the Wadi Khabila, which runs for twelve kilometers (about eight miles), until it reaches the paved road. The track is well marked, but one needs a good four-wheel drive vehicle to get through some of the tougher spots.

81 top
The mangrove oasis of Nabq is considered to be the northernmost site in which Avicenia marina *grows; this plant is found in the area that extends from the Indian Ocean to the Red Sea.*

81 bottom A small hut made out of palm fronds and fibers, constitutes an excellent shelter for the few fishermen who live in the area around Nabq. During *the fishing season, some of the fish that are caught are salted and laid out to dry on the roofs of these huts, and are then stored for use during the winter.*

PRATICAL INFORMATION

In order to follow the itineraries described here, one should have a good four-wheel drive vehicle, which can be rented with or without a driver at Sharm el-Sheikh (there are rental agencies at the Mövenpick, Hilton, and Ghazala hotels).
Those who may want the help of a Bedouin guide, which is advisable for those with no experience of desert outings, can contact the Camel Dive Club (at the Sharm Mall Shopping Center) or the Tourist Village of Shark Bay (plan on spending about fifty Egyptian pounds per day).
Lastly, for the less adventuresome, there are numerous agencies which will arrange organized excursions, with a four-wheel drive vehicle, a driver, and a guide.

STRAIT OF TIRAN

The strait of Tiran, which closes off the Gulf of Eilat to the south, is bounded by the coast of the Sinai peninsula and the coast of Saudi Arabia. At the center of the strait is the island of Tiran, flanked to the east by the little island of Sanafir.

The area of the strait of Tiran is enormously important in military terms, and one cannot land on either of the two islands - which belong to Saudi Arabia but are "on loan" to Egypt. It is possible, however, to make a number of enchanting dives in various sites along the southeastern coast of Tiran and on the coral reefs that bound it to the northwest; these reefs are considered to be the loveliest and best preserved in the entire Sharm region.

Four coral reefs occupy the center of the strait: Gordon Reef, to the north; Jackson Reef, to the south; and two other smaller reefs, Thomas Reef and Woodhouse Reef, in the center.

All of these coral reefs are favorite diving spots for the many scuba divers who favor this stretch of sea, less popular than the waters off Ras Mohammed. In these sites, the fauna is extremely abundant and tends to be pelagic, and it is quite common to sight large fish and sharks; the presence of powerful currents can make diving in the Strait of Tiran quite demanding.

82 top Sinuous coral whips and undulating alcyonarians provide a spectacular natural setting for a scuba diver.

82 bottom Of the four reefs that lie lengthwise along the Strait of Tiran, Gordon Reef is the southernmost. On this coral reef, one can see the wreck of a ship

that ran aground on the northern side, and, to the south, a small lighthouse which marks the navigable channel. At top, one can see the small Thomas Reef.

83 top left
An overall view of the island of Tiran, with the deep bay: this entire area, of great strategic importance, is still subjected to a wide array of military regulations, and because of its importance to naturalists, has been incorporated in the National Park of Ras Mohammed.

83 bottom left
Encouraged in their growth by the powerful currents that sweep across the seabeds here, alcyonarians and gorgonians cover the walls of the reef.

83 top right
The depths of the island of Tiran serve as a backdrop to the wreck of a freighter that ran aground on the coral shallows of the Gordon Reef.

83 bottom right
The waves break on the reef where underwater life pulsates frenetically, featuring all of the main species of coral fish abound.

83 bottom right
Swimming along just a few meters below the surface, one has the impression of being in an authentic garden of corals, in which umbrellas of acropora alternate with vast areas of fire coral and large coral formations.

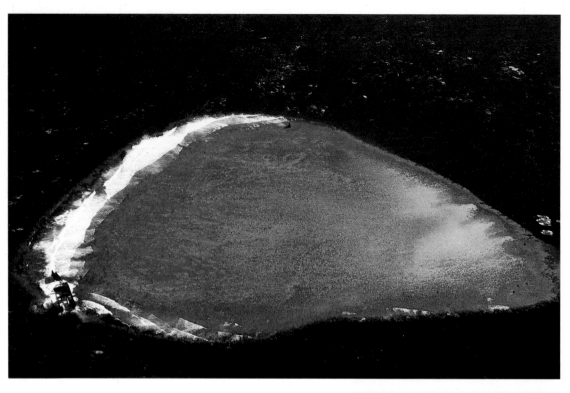

84 top On the coral banks of Jackson Reef, the northernmost reef in the strait of Tiran, one can also find the wreck of a freighter, which ran aground on the shallows of the northern slope, in a position parallel to that of the freighter that lies on Gordon Reef.

84 center left A numerous school of barracudas (Sphyraena qenie) swims through the water in close ranks, following the flow of the currents.

84 center right The strait of Tiran, with its coral reefs, is one of the most popular destinations of the scuba divers of Naama Bay.

84 bottom left Jacks (Caranx sp.) are powerful swimmers that feed on smaller fish, and they generally hunt in a school; nonetheless it is not uncommon to see large specimens patrolling solo along the walls of the reef, in search of prey.

84 bottom right The colors of the sponges and corals that grow on the wall of the reef merge to create an unusual and harmonious whole — a palette of colors worthy of the world's finest painters.

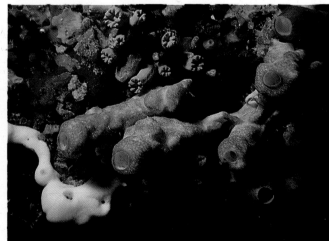

85 top The saber squirrelfish (Sargocentron spiniferum) *often shows a fairly aggressive nature, especially when required to defend its territory from possible intruders, whether they be other fish or scuba divers.*

85 center Of the many families of alcyonarians, the most common in the waters of the Red Sea is without a doubt that of the nephteids, distinguished by an unbelievable variety of shades of color.

85 bottom A giant sea fan extends from the coral wall, extending in a number of branches toward the open waters.

FROM NAAMA BAY TO DAHAB

Between the paved road that runs from Sharm el-Sheikh to Dahab and the coast of the Gulf of Eilat, there extends a territory that is marked by wadis running northeast, emptying into the sea and covered with broad expanses of detritus and earth. The mountains here are not very high, reaching a maximum altitude of one thousand eighty meters (3,542 feet) with the Gebel Qnai. Often the peaks of crumbling granite and the flanks of the hills are smooth and uniform, worn away by atmospheric agents that have softened and rounded their shapes. The succession of hills are occasionally interrupted by the long dark intrusions of the volcanic dikes, which cut vertically up and down the rock faces, or else run parallel with them like a border or hem. Acacias, thorny capers, succulents, and desert melons are not uncommon in this area, and a brief thundershower is enough to cause the vegetation to turn a bright vibrant green. When the season allows a bit of pasturage for the livestock, then there spring up numerous Beduin villages and encampments. The landscape of rocks and broad valleys of sand is often enlivened by small caravans of Beduins riding on dromedaries and by herds of black goats watched over by women or children. The infrequent buildings and the encampments along the road indicate sand quarries which serve mostly to provide raw materials for the manufacture of cement and glass.

Itinerary
At a distance of about three kilometers (about two miles) past Naama Bay, first one will find on the right the road that leads down to the tourist resort of Sheikh Coast (Coral Bay) and then, three kilometers (about two miles) further along, a track that leads down to Shark Bay, where there is a group of bungalows and a diving center. A third track, just one kilometer (about a thousand yards) further on, leads to the underwater site of Wichita Falls. Next comes an Egyptian

checkpoint: and if one continues along the road running parallel to the coast, another four kilometers (about two-and-a-half miles) of travel brings one to the international airport of Ras Nasrani; if, instead, one turns left and passes through the checkpoint, the road continues toward Dahab, running through the mountains in a northeasterly direction, and then climbing toward the pass of Sharira. At 55.5 kilometers (about thirty-five miles), at the Sharira Pass. At a distance of fifty kilometers, or thirty miles, on the left is the mouth of the Wadi Madsus, Wadi Shetan, Wadi Shellal, Wadi Nasb, Oasis of Nasb; a small pyramid-shaped monument has been built on the left, in memory of an Israeli engineer working on these roads, who was killed by a mine. At sixty-three kilometers (about forty miles), one will note on the right the track that leads off to Wadi Qnai el-Rayan (see itinerary) and, another 1.3 kilometers (just under a mile) further on, a second, wider track leading slightly downhill; this second track leads to Wadi Qnai el-Atschan (see itinerary), taking one to the Red Sea coast close to Dahab, running through an enormous ravine bounded by tall rocky cliff walls. At a distance of eighty kilometers (about fifty miles) past the checkpoint, one comes to a fork in the road: if one takes the left-hand turning, the road continues along toward Nuweiba; if one goes to the right, one descends to Dahab. At a distance of three kilometers (about two miles) past this intersection, just before entering Dahab, a track begins on the right, and is marked by a sign. This track leads to Wadi Connection and to Rest Valley Mountain (see itinerary). After this, on the left, one will find an asphalt road leading north that links up directly to the track that goes to the famous diving sites of Canyon and Blue Hole. If one continues straight ahead in an easterly direction, one passes a second asphalt road that leads to the village of Assalah, and a few hundred meters (yards) further on is Dahab.

86 and 87 top A cascade of exceedingly fine, golden-yellow sand, the product of wind- and weather-erosion of the striated rocks along the road leading to Dahab, provides a remarkable sight. The place name Dahab, in the Beduin language, in fact, means "gold."

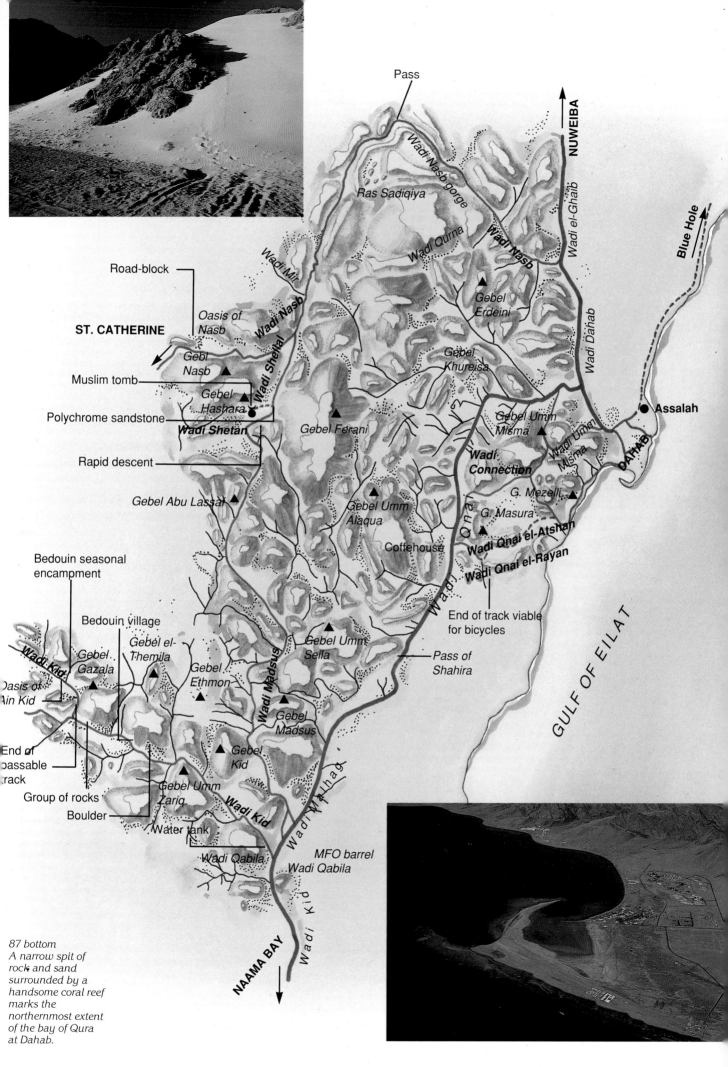

Pass

NUWEIBA

Blue Hole

Wadi Nasb gorge

Ras Sadiqiya

Wadi Qurna

Wadi Nasb

Wadi el-Ghaib

▲ *Gebel Erdeini*

Road-block

Wadi Mir

Oasis of Nasb

ST. CATHERINE

Wadi Nasb

Wadi Dahab

Gebel Khureisa

Gebl Nasb ▲

Muslim tomb

Wadi Shellal

▲ *Gebel Hashara* ▲

● **Assalah**

Polychrome sandstone

Wadi Shetan

Gebel Ferani ▲

Gebel Umm Misma ▲

Wadi Connection

Wadi Umm Misma

DAHAB

Rapid descent

Gebel Abu Lassal ▲

G. Mezelli ▲

Gebel Umm Alaqua ▲

G. Masura

▲ **Wadi Qnai el-Atshan**

Coffehouse

Wadi Qnai

Wadi Qnai el-Rayan

Bedouin seasonal encampment

End of track viable for bicycles

Bedouin village

Gebel el-Themila ▲

▲ *Gebel Umm Seila*

Wadi Kid

Gebel Gazala ▲

Gebel Ethmon ▲

Wadi Madsus

— Pass of Shahira

Oasis of Ain Kid

GULF OF EILAT

Gebel Madsus ▲

End of passable track

▲ *Gebel Kid*

Group of rocks

▲ *Gebel Umm Zarig*

Boulder

Wadi Kid

Water tank

Wadi Malhaq

Wadi Qabila

MFO barrel
Wadi Qabila

Wadi Kid

NAAMA BAY

87 bottom
A narrow spit of rock and sand surrounded by a handsome coral reef marks the northernmost extent of the bay of Qura at Dahab.

WADI MADSUS - WADI SHETAN - WADI SHELLAL - WADI NASB - OASIS OF NASB

The truly adventurous will appreciate this itinerary, which covers more than ninety kilometers (nearly sixty miles) of track, running through wadis that are still unknown to most tourists. This is an excursion that can be covered in a single day, if one sets out early in the morning, or else in two half-day trips, with an overnight stay in the oasis of Wadi Nasb. Because there is a six hundred meter (about two thousand feet) stretch of extremely steep road, one would be well advised to run this itinerary from north to south as described, so that this steep slope is in descent, and to use first or second gear in one's 4x4 car.

Itinerary

From the Egyptian military checkpoint at the beginning of the Wadi Madsus, on the left of the paved road, one drives for a distance of 42.6 kilometers (about twenty-seven miles). It is easy to recognize Wadi Madsus because of the presence of an orange and white barrel belonging to the MFO which marks the beginning of the track; this barrel stands only one kilometer (about half a mile) past the stretch of Wadi Kid that runs to the left of the paved road. Vegetation is extremely sparse, each curve is just like the last one and the imposing mountains march one after the other in repetition. Along the side of the track, one can encounter rudimentary heliports marked by white stones and utilized by the MFO - at a distance of four kilometers (two-and-a-half miles) from the beginning of the wadi on the right of the road and at a distance of twelve kilometers (seven-and-a-half miles) on the left, although these are not permanent locations. At a distance of nineteen kilometers (about twelve miles) from the beginning of the wadi, one begins to encounter the first ravines, which continue for another kilometer (about half a mile); then the mountains spread apart, extending their slopes dotted with greenish and purplish stones down into the valley. The track ends on the left in a observation terrace that overlooks the Wadi Shellal below, while on the right the track continues in a steep descent that should be driven with extreme

88 top The Wadi Madsus, a harsh and wild valley with scanty vegetation, ends in a daunting plunge down to the Wadi Shellal below.
In this picture, it is possible to see one of the many basalt dikes that interrupt the granite formations in numerous points.

88 bottom
The small oasis of the Wadi Shetan, in which one can see a remarkable waterfall, is located at the mouth of the Wadi Shellal, just a few hundred meters from the track.

care. At the end of the descent, one comes face to face with a formation of sandstone with bright colors that are unusual for this area (yellow, red, purple, ocher, and blue-grey). After making the dangerous descent, a few more meters will bring one to a Beduin tomb of a holy man, with its dome-shaped roof surmounted by a wrought-iron crescent moon. Setting out from the tomb, one can climb the small Wadi Shetan and reach, after about fifteen minutes of walking, a magnificent waterfall where the Beduins often bring their herds to drink. If one returns to the main track that follows Wadi Nasb along its sandy winding course, after about six kilometers (four miles) one will come to a fork; take the left-hand track and one will enter Wadi Nasb, which gives its name to the main valley. Eight kilometers (five miles) later, one will reach a oasis covered with gardens and palm trees. This tributary of Wadi Nasb is rich in vegetation: wild capers, mustard plants, bushes with a brilliant green color all bloom and flourish along the rocky walls like so many decorations. After so many kilometers (miles) of hostile desert, this hidden oasis will seem like a mirage. Immediately following the oasis, a checkpoint of the Egyptian army will halt anyone who does not have special permit from the military authorities from continuing along all the way to Saint Catherine. Those who do possess the special permit can continue along the track, which runs along amongst sandstone formations, finally fetching up in the general area of Saint Catherine, and specifically, in the Blue Desert. And returning to the main branch of Wadi Nasb, at its confluence with Wadi Shellal, and heading northeast, one continues for another sixteen kilometers (ten miles) across a broad plain: then the track runs through a pass and turns to the right amidst barbed-wire enclosures, and then begins an entrancing run through canyons with rock walls and ravines, where the magmatic changes color continuously, shifting from pink to red, from grey to light blue. After admiring these rock formations, one reaches the paved road from Nuweiba to Sharm at 6.7 kilometers (four miles) from the fork leading to Dahab.

89 top
A magnificent view of the Wadi Shellal appears to visitors who look out from the rock balcony that marks the end of the Wadi Madsus.

89 center right
The Wadi Shellal joins up with the majestic Wadi Nasb, one of the most important wadis in the Sinai peninsula: deep and lush in vegetation, it is a veritable river of sand, wending its way through a series of broad curves.

89 center left
The steep slope that runs from the end of the Wadi Madsus down to the Wadi Shellal below, should be descended with great caution.

89 bottom
At the mouth of the Wadi Shellal one encounters a small Islamic tomb, in which the remains of a holy man are buried.

DAHAB

Dahab is a site formed by a promontory that divides two Bays, Qura and Ghazala. In line with the Bay of Qura, which is protected to the north by the promontory of Dahab which curves around in a hook shape, is the large Holiday Village tourist complex.

The bay of Ghazala is broader and shallower than the Bay of Qura, and its shores are covered with an exceedingly fine golden-yellow sand that seems to have been the source of the name Dahab, a word that means "gold" in the Beduin tongue.

An extensive palm grove - one of the loveliest in the entire Sinai peninsula - borders the beach of Ghazala, helping to create a landscape of great beauty; the one fly in the ointment,

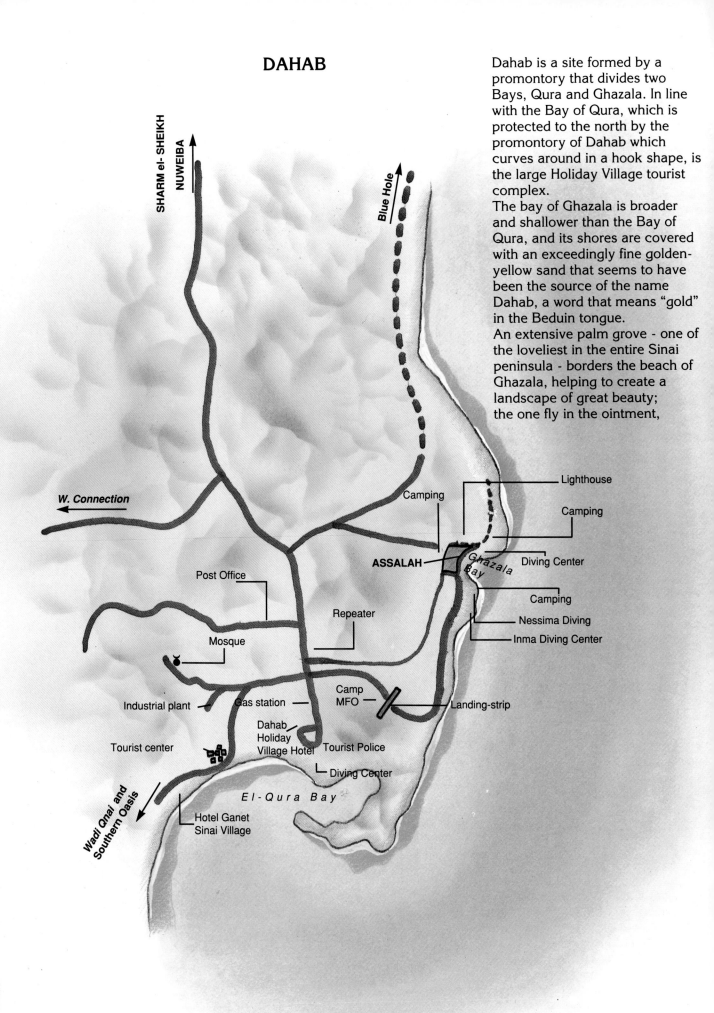

SHARM el- SHEIKH
NUWEIBA

Blue Hole

W. Connection

Camping

ASSALAH

Ghazala Bay

Lighthouse

Camping

Diving Center

Camping

Nessima Diving

Inma Diving Center

Post Office

Repeater

Mosque

Industrial plant

Gas station

Camp MFO

Landing-strip

Tourist center

Dahab Holiday Village Hotel

Tourist Police

Diving Center

Wadi Qnai and Southern Oasis

Hotel Ganet Sinai Village

El-Qura Bay

however, is the unconstrained development of the Beduin village of Assalah.

The local Beduins have been extremely canny in exploiting the resort potential of their site ever since the period of Israeli occupation, and have built a vast number of camp grounds, little restaurants, unassuming hotels, bars, and nightclubs along the bay. A crowded and motley array of human fauna frequents Assalah, and from a small Beduin village it has been transformed into a sort of alternative Sharm el-Sheikh teeming with globe-trotters with sleeping bags, who seem to have no fear of the fleas, lice, and well developed colonies of microbes and viruses that have found an ideal habitat in this site.

91 top In the bay of Ghazala, at Dahab, one finds the Beduin village of Assalah.

91 center left The beach, with its tall palm trees, is a place of great beauty. Despite the crowding, it has not yet been entirely overrun by tourism and construction.

91 center right The village of Assalah is one of the loveliest sites along the eastern coast of the Sinai, the destination of numerous tourists in search of authentic folkways, largely vanished elsewhere.

91 bottom Along the beach, Beduins with their camels await the arrival of new tourists.

WADI QNAI EL-RAYAN
Itinerary

The distance between Sharira Pass and the track that follows the bed of Wadi Qnai el-Rayan (the "wadi that irrigates") is 7.4 kilometers (under five miles). The track is well marked, and cuts off from the asphalt road, penetrating directly amongst the rock cliffs. Immediately on the right is a basalt dike that cuts straight up and down through the vertical extent of the colored granite. The wadi is relatively green, and there are many acacia trees. The track can accommodate a jeep for a distance of about two-and-a-half kilometers (about a mile-and-a-half), but it then breaks off. One can continue on foot along a trail that is clearly marked by the hoofprints of livestock. This is a good opportunity for a fairly easy hike. One can have the jeep taken back to the asphalt road

miles) from the Sharira Pass. Another point that can be taken as a landmark is a Beduin coffee shop, a cement building on the left some seven hundred meters (2,300 feet) from the track that cuts off on the right from the asphalt road. The track is well marked, and runs 8.5 kilometers (over five miles) toward the coast. In any case, one is advised to make use of an all-terrain vehicle, as there are some stretches of very deep sand. At first the road cuts across a level plain, surrounded by round-topped hills cut by veins of basalt that seem to be invading the lighter granite. Then the wadi narrows until a point in which the rocky cliff walls form a narrow canyon, and then open out again overlooking the sea. Here jeep tracks intersect and become muddled; the terrain however presents no particular difficulty, and all one need

92 The Wadi Qnai el-Atshan narrows in its final stretch, before running down to the sea, forming an impressive gorge.

leading to Dahab, where it can reach the coastal track and wait there for the hikers when the emerge from the other end of the wadi. In fact, both Wadi Qnai el-Rayan and Wadi Qnai el-Atschan run down to the coast.

WADI QNAI EL-ATSCHAN
Itinerary

The track of Wadi Qnai el-Atschan ("The thirsty one") runs off to the right from the asphalt road, at a distance of 8.7 kilometers (over five

to do is drive toward the coast; along the way at some point one will certainly encounter the track that leads to Dahab off on one's left. Along this track many hotels are springing up. Worth noting on the left is a piece of vernacular architecture - a laborers' house, covered and decorated with empty beer bottles. The track turns into an asphalt road, and on the right one begins to see the first houses of Dahab, hidden amongst the palm groves.

93 top and center
The upper section of the Wadi Qnai el-Atshan, is lush and verdant; the large mustard bushes are quite common.

93 bottom
While there is a good track that runs through the Wadi Qnai el-Atshan, the nearby Wadi Qnai el-Rayan can only be traversed on foot or by camel: the wadis merge at the southern coast of Dahab.

WADI CONNECTION - REST VALLEY MOUNTAIN

94 top The hike to the so-called Wadi Connection, immediately inland from Dahab, allows one to observe a landscape of enormous beauty.

94 bottom If one follows the easy track that splits off from the paved road just prior to Dahab, indicated by a sign reading "Wadi Connection," one will reach a great clearing where the Beduin have built a small rest-house, very popular on summer evenings.

Itinerary

Just a few kilometers (miles) outside of Dahab, in the open desert in an uncultivated wadi, there is restaurant-coffeeshop that is truly unusual; here one can also, if needed, spend the night in a cheerful and singular atmosphere. This is Rest Valley Mountain, which can be the destination of an easy drive by car (the track is accessible to all sorts of automobile) as well as a starting point for other excursions on foot or by camel into the mountains that tower on all sides. At a distance of three kilometers (about two miles) from the asphalt road from Sharm el-Sheikh to Nuweiba, after taking the fork in the road that leads to Dahab, one takes the well-beaten track that cuts off to the right from the road that leads to Dahab. This well-beaten track is marked by a sign reading "Wadi Connection - Rest Valley Mountain 5 km." The track that follows the bed of the Wadi Umm Misma climbs just slightly, and after about four kilometers (just over two miles) it splits in two: on the left it continues for about three kilometers (about two miles), running in the direction of Wadi Qnai el-Atschan, while after about a kilometer, or about a thousand yards, on the right it leads to the huts of the rest house, which is located in a broad level plain surrounded by mountains. This is the starting point for a number of tracks, one of which - cutting off to the left - leads directly to the Sharm-Nuweiba road. Often this track is impossible to use because of its very sandy surface. This track, about a kilometer, or about a thousand yards, from its start, makes a sharp turn to the left, and then leads to three different wells at three different elevations. This is a watering point used by the Beduins year-round for their livestock and for household purposes. All around the wells there is a luxuriant growth of greenery; the most impressive form of plant life here are the vivid green mustard bushes, with their oblong red fruit, bursting with seeds. After returning toward Dahab along the track of Wadi Umm Misma, one can enjoy a remarkable view of a landscape in which the prevailing color is the golden-yellow of the sandstone rocks that cover the wadi. This lovely hue contrasts perfectly with the intense blue of the Gulf of Eilat , bounded to the east by the corona of mountains that mark Saudi Arabia.

95 top right
Great bushes of colocynth (Cytrullus colocynthis), a member of Cucurbitaceae distinguished by its round yellow fruit, also known as "desert melon," are quite common in the area around the Wadi Connection. The Arabs call both plant and fruit, which resemble nothing so much as oranges, "handal" and they use it as an intestinal purge.

95 top left
After continuing past the rest-house and descending along the wadi which leads to three wells used by the Beduins to water their flocks, one can see a deep cleft in the granite that froms the eastern flank of the wadi.

95 center
Scattered shrubs and scanty vegetation are distinctive features of the landscape along the track that leads to the Wadi Connection.

95 bottom
The preparation of unleavened bread (aesh) in Beduin camps is still done according to the most traditional of methods.

DAHAB - BLUE HOLE

Itinerary

Just before entering Dahab, one may notice on the left a paved road heading north; when this road reaches the end of the village of Assalah, it becomes a track with a solid and well-beaten surface. After travelling for about eight kilometers (five miles) parallel to the coast, one reaches a diving center, alongside a coffee shop and restaurant.

This is the underwater site known as The Canyon (see diving sites). The track goes on past the diving center for about a kilometer; then the road surface is interrupted by

*96 top
The renowned Blue Hole, one of the most famous (and dangerous) diving sites in the Sinai peninsula, lies about eight kilometers (five miles) north of Dahab, and can be reached overland along a track that will accommodate all sorts of vehicles. Cars must stop, however, at about a kilometer's (three-quarters-of-a-mile's) distance, because of a landslide that has obstructed the road.*

damage caused by a landslide. From here, it is necessary to continue on foot along the shore of a large bay. At the southern tip of this bay is perhaps the best known of all the diving sites in the entire Sinai: the Blue Hole, so-called because the clear blue waters of the coral platform shade into a darker, midnight blue over a round and deep crater.

This point marks the beginning of the Park of Ras Abu Galum; it can be reached by car if one takes the track from Nuweiba.

96 center Almost entirely surrounded by coral reef, the Blue Hole drops down to a depth of some eighty meters (260 feet), and communicates with the open sea through a broad opening located at a depth of sixty-two meters (203 feet).

*96 bottom
Adorned with alcyonarians, sponges, and corals of every shape and color, the walls of the reef offer a sight of remarkable beauty.*

97 left A sea star perches upon the delicate branches of a gorgonian: the bright red of its coloring creates a remarkable chromatic contrast.

97 top right During the daylight hours, the coral polyps tend to remain closed, while by night they open to capture the microrganisms on which they feed.

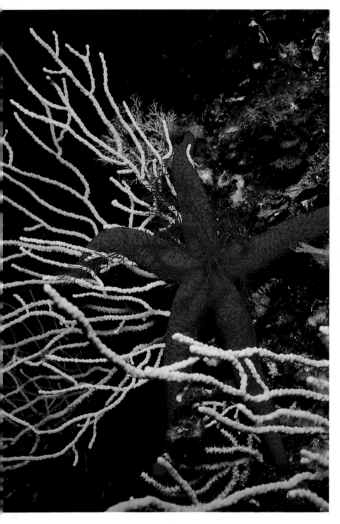

97 center right Coral groupers (Cephalopholis miniata) *and onespotted snappers* (Lutjanus monostigma) *fight for living space along the coral reef.*

97 bottom right A clownfish (Amphiprion bicinctus) *shows off its distinctive orange coloring crossed by two distinct vertical white bands.*

Scuba diving sites

At Dahab, there are a number of interesting places to dive; they can be broken down into two groups. The first group lies to the south of the Holiday Village; the second group lies to the north. All of these sites can be reached by land, but it is also possible to rent a boat at the local diving center in order to reach them by sea.

A Southern sites

1) Southern Oasis
This is a site set near a small group of palms on the beach, a little way south of the mouth of the Wadi Qnai el-Atschan. One can get here over land by taking the track that starts just north of the Holiday Village and runs along the sea shore. Upon a sandy bottom, which is in some points as much as forty meters (one hundred thirty feet) deep, tower coral pinnacles.

2) The Caves
A little site of the Southern Oasis are The Caves, on a bay near a pile of stones that marks their position.

B Northern sites

1) The Lighthouse
Located near the lighthouse of Dahab (in the northern section of the bay of Assalah), this dive allows one to admire a wall of coral that descends to a depth of between twenty-five and thirty meters (eighty and a hundred feet).

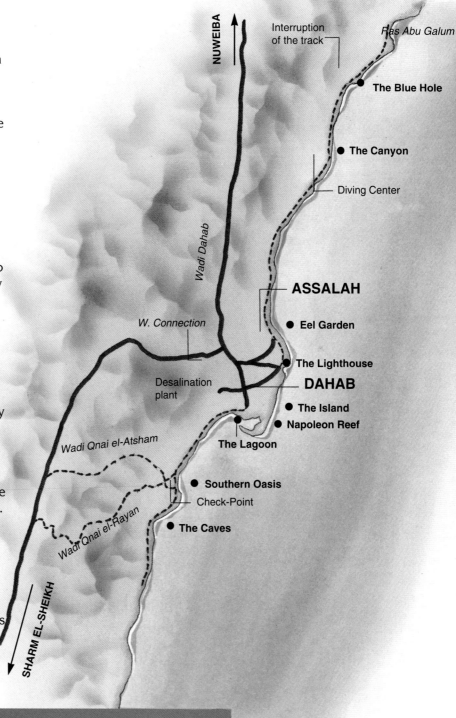

98 Just before reaching the Blue Hole, one encounters another very popular diving site: the Canyon. A diving center and a coffee shop are located quite close by.

2) Eel Garden

Corresponding with the northernmost group of palm trees of the village of Assalah after the lighthouse that marked the location of the previous site, Eel Garden is a shallow reef upon which a great many small eels swim.

3) The Canyon

One can reach this site, which is considered to be one of the most interesting along the coast between Sharm and Nuweiba, by following the beaten-earth track that leads to Blue Hole (see the itinerary from Dahab to Blue Hole). Here the reef forms a huge lagoon, interrupted by a number of channels; after swimming through the channel on the right and exiting it, one must head north for another twenty meters (sixty-six feet). One will see a pinnacle rising from the seabed and, behind it, a deep fissure that runs down to a depth of forty-nine meters (one hundred sixty feet), which should only be explored by very experienced divers.

4) The Blue Hole

Set just two kilometers (about a mile-and-a-half) to the north of The Canyon, the Blue Hole is perhaps the best-known, and the most dangerous site on the Sinai coast of the Gulf of Eilat
It is a crater that opens in the coral reef, dropping down to a depth of eighty meters (two hundred sixty-two feet), while there is a passage to the open sea through the reef in the form of a broad arch at a depth of sixty-two meters (two hundred three feet).
Only experienced divers should explore it. It is also interesting just to explore the edges, where the depth of the lagoon is no greater than one-and-a-half meters (five feet), and the typical reef fauna is particularly abundant.

99 top left
Here too the coral seabeds are particularly rich in the fauna and flora that are typical of the Red Sea.

99 bottom left
A banner butterflyfish (Heniochus diphreutes), in the foreground, and a masked butterflyfish (Chaetodon semilarvatus) swim together in transparent blue water.

99 top right
The large gorgonian sea fans are one of the most distinctive features of the Red Sea.

99 bottom right
A group of blotch-eye soldierfish (Myripristis murdjan) enlivens the seabed with red; this species, which is essentially nocturnal by habit, remains close to the reef by day, just before the mouths of underwater grottoes, where it can take shelter if threatened.

DAHAB - NUWEIBA - TABA

After passing the intersection with the road that leads down to Dahab, another ten-and-a-half kilometers (six-and-a-half miles) of driving brings one to a track, cutting off to the right, that leads to the area of the Natural Park of Ras Abu Galum (see itinerary), and then thirty-eight kilometers (about twenty-four miles) later, one reaches the intersection of the excellent road that leads to Saint Catherine, eighty-five kilometers (fifty-three miles) away. Further on, at a distance of forty-five kilometers (twenty-eight miles) from Dahab, the road rises over a second pass and - after a panoramic observation point - begins to drop and to head in an easterly direction. Just before a group of large tanks on the left, one can see the mouth of Wadi Saada, and the beginning of the track that leads to Ain Khudra (see itinerary); if one continues along the paved road, however, one reaches the great bay from which one sees all of Nuweiba. From this point, the road heads north, after an intersection with the road that splits off toward the oasis of Nuweiba-Muzeina, site of the great tourist resort of the Sayaddin Beach Hotel and, a little further north, the harbor. Continuing northward, after two kilometers (just over a mile), one comes to the first gas station while, on the right, there is a road that leads to the harbor of Nuweiba; another three kilometers (two

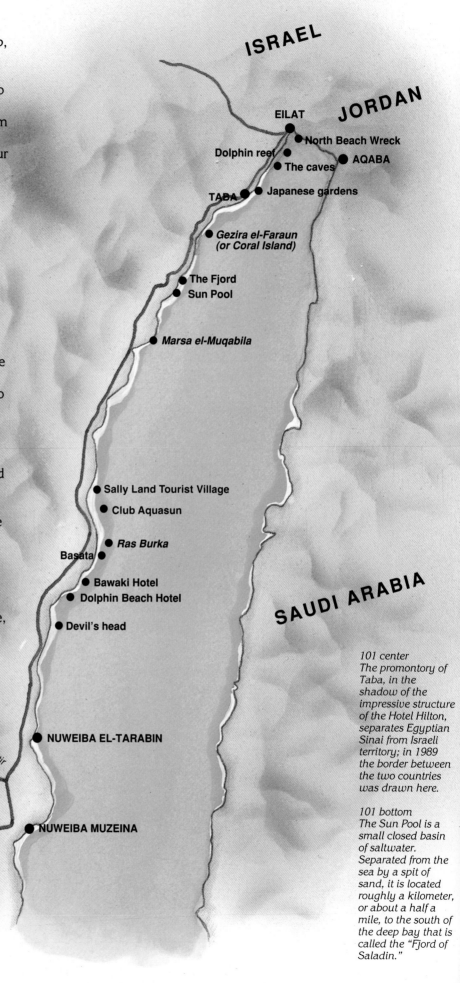

101 top Nuweiba is made up of two centers: Nuweiba Muzeina to the south, and Nuweiba el-Tarabin to the north. At Nuweiba Muzeina the port facilities are located (a ferryboat runs daily between here and the Jordanian coast), along with a number of tourist villages. In the area around Nuweiba el-Tarabin live the Beduins of the tribe of the Tarabin, who gave the region its name.

101 center The promontory of Taba, in the shadow of the impressive structure of the Hotel Hilton, separates Egyptian Sinai from Israeli territory; in 1989 the border between the two countries was drawn here.

101 bottom The Sun Pool is a small closed basin of saltwater. Separated from the sea by a spit of sand, it is located roughly a kilometer, or about a half a mile, to the south of the deep bay that is called the "Fjord of Saladin."

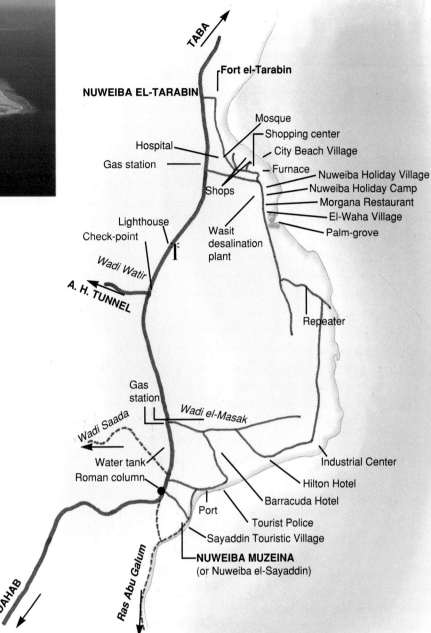

miles) brings one to the paved road, on the left, that leads to the Tunnel Ahmed Hamdi via Wadi Watir (see itinerary). Three kilometers (two miles) further along - at a distance of seventy kilometers, or about forty-five miles, from Dahab - there is another gas station at the same point in the road as the road that leads down to the coast and toward the center of Nuweiba and the Nuweiba Holiday Village. Continuing toward the north, in the direction of Taba, the road begins to climb; on the right is a detour that leads to the Beduin village and the fortress of Tarabin. Another twelve kilometers further on one reaches the diving site known as Devil's Head, distinguished by a large boulder; four kilometers (two-and-a-half miles) further on is the Dolphin Beach Hotel and another two kilometers (one-and-a-half miles) past that is the Bawaki Hotel. One then passes Ras el-Burqa, where the camp ground of Basata is located (ninety-three kilometers, or fifty-eight miles, past Dahab), and then Club Aquasun, the little oasis where the Sally Land Tourist Village has been set up (ninety-eight kilometers, or sixty-one miles, past Dahab), and then, finally, the diving site of Marsa el-Muqabila (one hundred thirteen kilometers, or seventy-one miles, past Dahab). After passing this point, the road splits off from the coast for six kilometers, or four miles, turning back down to meet the coast near two spectacular spots: the Sun Pool and the Fjord (one hundred nineteen kilometers, or seventy-four miles, past Dahab). Lastly, another five kilometers (three miles) further

along, one comes to Pharaoh's Island, known as *Gezira el-Faraun* in Arabic, and also called Coral Island, which is linked with the mainland by a ferry service. After Pharaoh's Island, another five kilometers (three miles) brings one to Taba, and the Israeli border (one hundred thirty-three kilometers, or eighty-three miles, past Dahab).

102 top left
At Nuweiba el-Tarabin is a major fortress built in the sixteenth century by the Mameluke sultan Ashraf el-Ghuri to protect passing caravans and, at the same time, to defend the territory from invasion. The fortress was later rebuilt under the Ottoman Empire in the eighteenth century; the Ottomans wished to make safe their shipping in the waters of the Red Sea.

102 top right
On the interior of the fortress is a well used frequently by the Beduins that live in the area to water their animals.

102 center left
This deep inlet with its turquoise-blue water, set amidst rocky granite shores, and known as the "Fjord," is one of the loveliest spots along the coast between Nuweiba and Taba, and it is located just a few kilometers, or miles, from the renowned "Island of the Pharaoh."

102 center right
The castle of Coral Island built by Crusaders at the beginning of the twelfth century upon the remains of a Byzantine settlement, it was later enlarged by the sultan Salah al-Din, or Saladin, who seized the island in 1182.

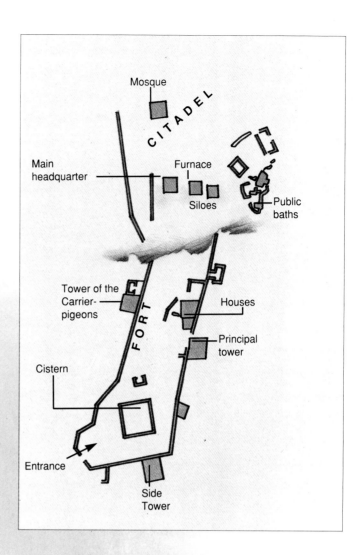

Mosque

CITADEL

Main
headquarter

Furnace

Siloes

Public
baths

FORT

Tower of the
Carrier-
pigeons

Houses

Principal
tower

Cistern

Entrance

Side
Tower

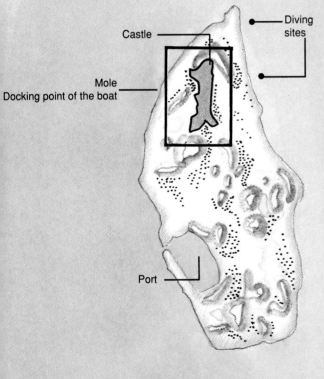

Diving
sites

Castle

Mole

Docking point of the boat

Port

THE ISLAND
OF THE
PHARAOH

102 bottom
The Island of the
Pharaoh, called
Geziret Faraun *in*
Arabic, is situtated
just a few hundred
meters, or yards,
from the coast.
It is believed to the
ancient Phoenician
port of Eziongaber,
founded by the

king Hiram of Tyre
in the tenth
century B.C.
The island, also
called Coral Island
because of the
extensive coral
formations found
on its northeastern
coast, is
dominated by a
great castle.

DAHAB - NUWEIBA - SAINT CATHERINE

At a distance of thirty-eight kilometers (about twenty-four miles) from Dahab begins an excellent road that leads to Saint Catherine. The first part of the route runs uphill until a first pass; from the vantage point of this pass, after a sharp curve, one admire the magnificent landscape of Wadi Ghazala. From the pass, the road runs downhill for a while; at the end of the downhill stretch, on the left, there is a Beduin coffee shop and then, on the right, the beginning of the track that leads to the oasis of Ain Khudra (see itinerary). After passing through a double checkpoint, of the MFO and the Egyptian army, at a distance of eight kilometers (five miles) from the pass, one can see at about a kilometer (a thousand yards) on the right, a large free-standing rock with inscriptions in a number of languages: Nabataean, Greek, Roman, Byzantine, and from the period of the Crusades. This is called the Rock of

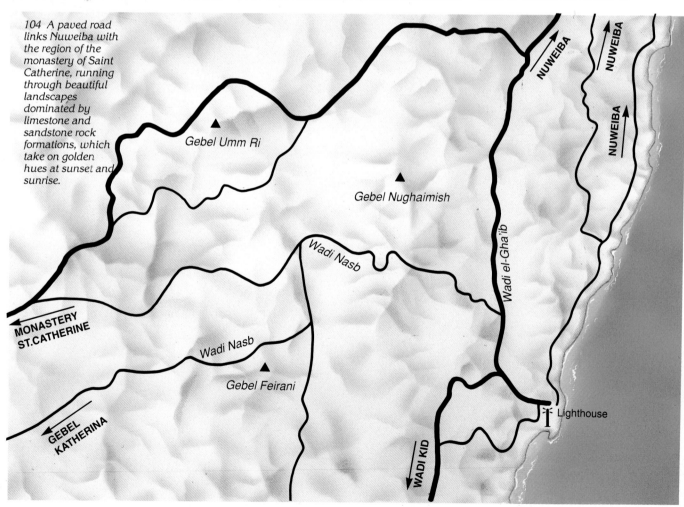

104 *A paved road links Nuweiba with the region of the monastery of Saint Catherine, running through beautiful landscapes dominated by limestone and sandstone rock formations, which take on golden hues at sunset and sunrise.*

Gebel Umm Ri

Gebel Nughaimish

Wadi Nasb

Wadi Nasb

NUWEIBA

NUWEIBA

NUWEIBA

Wadi el-Gha'ib

MONASTERY
ST.CATHERINE

Gebel Feirani

GEBEL
KATHERINA

WADI KID

Lighthouse

Inscriptions, while the locals call it *Haggar Maktub*, the "Written Stone." A brief stretch of easy track allows one to reach the rock. After passing the rock, leaving it behind one on the left, another seven hundred meters (2,300 feet) of track takes one to an outcropping of sandstone which marks the edge of the highland. One can climb to the peak of these rocks and look out over the Wadi Khudra; from here one can enjoy a grandiose panorama of the oasis of Ain Khudra; two-and-a-half hours of hiking will take one there. After returning to the paved road and travelling another five hundred meters (sixteen hundred feet), one will note on the left another track that leads, first, to a second free-standing rock, very similar to the "Written Stone," and covered with an abundance of graffiti: many of these writings depict animals that were present in the Sinai during prehistoric times. Then, four kilometers (two-and-a-half miles) further on, after passing a small Beduin settlement, one reaches an interesting complex of *Nawamis*, which can be reached by walking a few minutes from where one has left one's all-terrain vehicle.

The term *nawamis* is a Beduin word, meaning "flies," and is used to describe these prehistoric tombs found in the central Sinai: they are circular constructions made of dry-wall stone, with a door facing west.

After returning to the paved road, one can continue toward Saint Catherine.

*106 top
After passing the "Rock of Inscriptions," the track leads on to a scenic vantage-point called "Observation Point," from which one can look out over the Wadi Khudra, which runs quite nearly parallel to the larger Wadi Ghazala, and the oasis of Ain Khudra. A footpath allows one to walk to the oasis in about two hours.*

*106 center
The track that leads to "Observation Point," splitting off from the paved road that links Nuweiba with Saint Catherine, is increasingly frequented by tourists.*

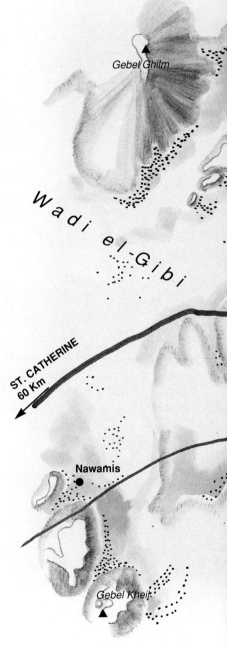

Gebel Ghilm

Wadi el-Gibi

ST. CATHERINE 60 Km

Nawamis

Gebel Kheil

*106 bottom
The Wadi Watir runs from the center of the Sinai to the coast, linking the region of Nuweiba with the little town of Nakhl in the central highlands. In the easternmost section of the Wadi Watir, the abundance of water coincides with areas of great beauty, and the wadi is adorned by many tufts of palm trees, standing alongside the road. From the Wadi Watir, three major tracks set out, leading respectively to the Colored Canyon, the oasis of Ain Khudra, and the oasis of Ain Umm Ahmed.*

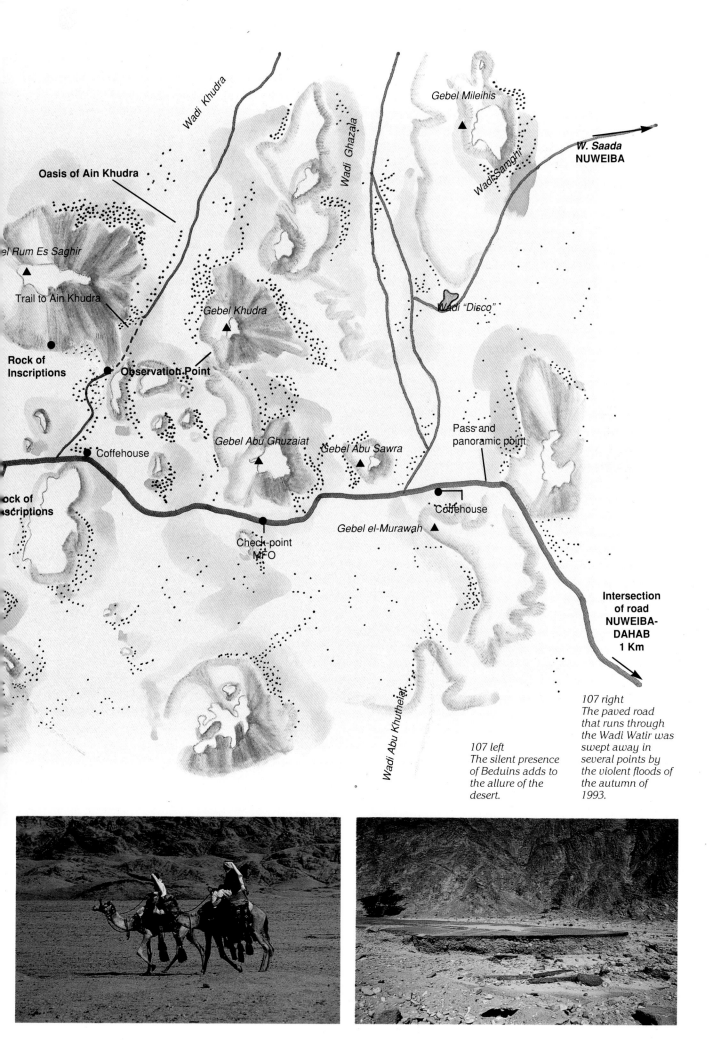

Oasis of Ain Khudra

Wadi Khudra

Gebel Mileihis

Wadi Ghazala

Wadi Samghir

W. Saada
NUWEIBA

el Rum Es Saghir

Trail to Ain Khudra

Rock of Inscriptions

Observation Point

Gebel Khudra

Wadi "Disco"

Coffehouse

Gebel Abu Ghuzaiat

Gebel Abu Sawra

Pass and panoramic point

ock of scriptions

Coffehouse

Check-point MFO

Gebel el-Murawah

Intersection of road NUWEIBA-DAHAB 1 Km

Wadi Abu Khutheiat

107 left
The silent presence of Beduins adds to the allure of the desert.

107 right
The paved road that runs through the Wadi Watir was swept away in several points by the violent floods of the autumn of 1993.

NUWEIBA MUZEINA

Port

Gebel Magnas

MFO barrel

Gebel Ummzerio

Wadi Rasasa

Track to
Nuweiba

ST. CATHERINE

Cisterns and bedouin village

DAHAB

Gebel Fergh

Gebel Sukhh

Track to
Nuweiba

Gebel Mikeimin

Narrow valley
of Wadi
Nasasa

Wadi Hooba

Gebel Rasasa

El-Qardud

Fishermen's
huts

**Track to
Blue Hole**

Ras Abu Galum

NATURAL PARK OF ABU GALUM

The natural park of Abu Galum, like its counterpart at Nabq, is part of the program to safeguard territory set forth by the authorities at the national park of Ras Mohammed. This is an entirely wild area both because it is distant from the places traditionally visited by hikers and because it occupies a strategic site and is therefore of interest to the military. Unfortunately, only recently have the authorities recognized the importance of the area of Abu Galum to the maintenance of an environmental equilibrium in the region; it is of equal importance to the Beduin population that lives in this area, and whose survival is almost entirely dependent upon the survival of the various species of fish found here. This delay has resulted in the uncontrolled accumulation of garbage of all kinds on most of the beaches, due to the frequent high seas and the carelessness of Beduins and of the crews of ships passing through the Gulf of Eilat. The park authorities are beginning to respond to the situation.

108 The coast of Ras Abu Galum is lined by a track that allows one to climb northward as far as Nuweiba or to descend southward toward Dahab, near the bay where the Blue Hole is located.

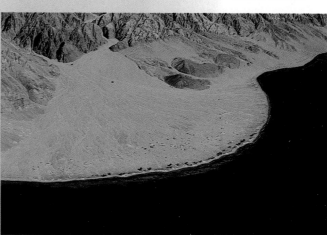

Itinerary

The track that leads to Abu Galum begins at a distance of ten-and-a-half kilometers (six-and-a-half miles) from the intersection between the road that leads to Saint Catherine and the road that from Dahab continues on to Nuweiba. It is marked on the right by a stretch of asphalt and a barrel painted white and orange; it runs nearly thirty kilometers (about twenty miles) to the sea. The track is well-beaten due to the regular passage of vans and lorries owned by the Beduins and of military vehicles of the MFO; there is a major MFO observation point in this area.

At a distance of six kilometers (four miles) from the beginning of the track, there is a Beduin village with a number of masonry houses and cisterns built to gather rainwater. A number of the houses are built against the rocks, and the enclosures of the gardens contain boulders with the odd shapes typical of sandstone eroded by the elements. This is a reasonably wealthy village: the cisterns ensure an adequate water supply all year round. Women and children guard the livestock and raise a few crops, while the men go down to the coast to fish. At a distance of about sixteen kilometers (ten miles) from the village, on the left, at the top of Gebel Sukhn, rises the antenna of the observation base of the MFO. The track is extremely steep at this point, and there are a number of difficult obstacles before reaching the pass and running along slightly downhill toward the sea. After an open, sandy stretch, the track heads sharply east (at twenty-seven kilometers, or seventeen miles from the beginning of the track) and runs through deep canyons and ravines. This landscape is at once harsh and - at the same time - fascinating, and every curve seems to conceal the final destination and to distract the traveller with the patterns and colors of the rocks. The wadi suddenly opens out over the sea in a flood of rubble and stones. A few hundred meters (yards) further along, and one reaches the track that runs along the coast and ends further south, after six kilometers (four miles), in a lovely little bay, ideal for a campsite, while toward the north the track continues for more than forty kilometers (twenty-five miles), until it reaches the little town of Nuweiba. Along the coastal route, there are two checkpoints manned by the Egyptian army, and it is necessary to show one's passport. In the winter, this area is subject to violent flooding, and the tracks may be interrupted or even eradicated entirely. If there have been recent heavy rainfalls, one should speak to park authorities before setting out.

109 top
The impressive Wadi Rasasa runs, with an east-west orientation, toward the coast just south of Nuweiba, not far from Ras Abu Galum. A well-marked track runs along the bed of the wadi, allowing one to reach the seashore.

109 center
The spectacular coastline around Ras Abu Galum has been declared a protected area and incorporated in the national park of Ras Mohammed; the entire area, not yet popular with tourists, has fortunately been subjected to strict regulation to protect its beauty and its wildlife.

109 bottom
In the area around Ras Abu Galum live a number of groups of Beduins who fish and cultivate small gardens.

110 top The wadi Rasasa is a wild valley that runs generally east-west and drops down to the sea, not far from Ras Abu Galum.

110 center A Beduin village with stone houses is crossed by the track that runs down from the Wadi Rasasa. A number of stone tanks allow the Beduins to gather water for the irrigation of orchards and small gardens.

110 bottom Near the village, a number of tents can still be seen, but the increasingly sedentary Beduins are abandoning this typical habitation of the desert peoples, which still survives chiefly as a tourist attraction.

111 top left
An encounter with Beduins on camelback is always an enormous thrill.

111 center right
A view along the track that follows the coast links Ras Abu Galum with Nuweiba.

111 center left
Ras Abu Galum is a site that abounds in fish and is frequented by local fishermen; during certain periods of the year they take up residence on the beach, building huts out of palm fronds, venturing out to sea in small fishing boats.

111 bottom
The coast of the Gulf of Eilat to the north of Dahab is distinguished by a fairly narrow littoral strip and by the presence of high mountains, intersected by a system of wadis, which run down to the waters of the Red Sea.

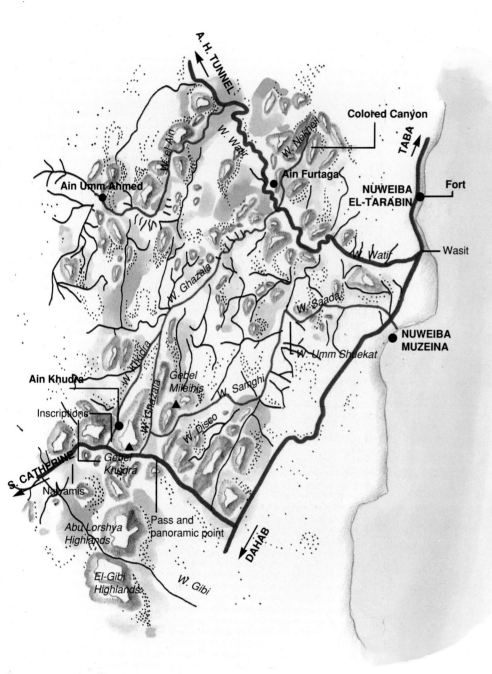

TRACK FROM NUWEIBA TO AIN KHUDRA (via Wadi Saada)

Before passing the group of cisterns on the left of the road from Nuweiba, there is a track, which climbs slightly through the Wadi Saada and leads to the magnificent oasis of Ain Khudra, which can also be reached via another track that begins at Ain Furtaga. After passing through a narrow and winding canyon that runs between high cliff walls - at a distance of ten kilometers, or about six miles, from the beginning of the track - one encounters a well, and then the track runs into the broad and sandy Wadi Samghi; this wadi has a great many acacia trees in its central area.

The Beduins sometimes call these trees "glue trees," with reference to the great quantity of red resin that they produce.

Then one reaches a line with Gebel Milehes, which can be seen off to the right, and at twenty-four kilometers (fifteen miles) from the beginning of the track one can admire an impressive formation of pink sandstone.

Beginning at this point, the sandstone becomes the distinctive feature of the landscape. These rocks draw one's attention both because of the remarkable colors generated by the presence of ferrous oxides and manganese and because of the remarkable shapes into which they are carved by wind, sand, and water. At twenty-nine kilometers (eighteen miles) from the beginning of the track, a giant sandstone boulder that stands near the wall of the wadi marks out a broad space that is used by the Beduins in their nocturnal feasts in the open desert, like some huge natural discotheque, to the point that the locals have dubbed it "wadi disco." About a kilometer (a little over half a mile) from this spot, one crosses the immense Wadi Ghazala entering it. At a distance of thirty-five kilometers (twenty-two miles) from the beginning of the track, it becomes necessary to stay on one's left, and to follow the compass bearing of 210 degrees in order to reach a point of view (thirty-seven kilometers, or about twenty-three miles), where it is possible to admire a handsome basalt mountain chain. Running along the sandy bed of the wadi, one arrives at last at the small but splendid Oasis of Ain Khudra, at distance of forty-four kilometers (twenty-seven and a half miles) from the beginning of the track. The green palms of the oasis contrast with the yellow and red of the sand and the sandstone, which is the predominant form of rock found in this region, one of the most beautiful areas in the Sinai. At Ain Khudra, there is a spring of exceedingly pure water, and a deep well, around which there is a small settlement of Beduins. After crossing the oasis, keep to the west, and follow the Wadi Ghazala; after sixteen kilometers (ten miles) one reaches the paved road that links Nuweiba and Saint Catherine.

NUWEIBA - WADI WATIR - TUNNEL AHMED HAMDI

A fork on the left situated just after the southernmost part of Nuweiba el-Tarabin marks the road that leads to the Tunnel under the Suez Canal, a drive of three hundred and thirty-eight kilometers (two hundred and eleven miles), for a considerable way running along the bed of the Wadi Watir. The rocky cliffs of this wadi are high and quite sheer, with long dark striations, and amidst such a harsh landscape it is surprising to find the handsome oasis of Ain Furtaga, a palm grove that stands about fifteen kilometers, or ten miles, past the fork in the road, on the edge of the paved road where often, in the middle of the summer, one can see water, moss, and little plants of an intense green hue.
From here, one can reach the well-known Colored Canyon (see route), or, by continuing another twenty kilometers, or twelve-and-a-half miles, along the road, one enter the track that leads to Ain Umm Ahmed (see route), one of the loveliest oases of the Sinai.

113 top An oil drum painted with the colors of the Egyptian flag marks the beginning of the track that leads to the Wadi Watir at Ain Khudra.

113 center and bottom The oasis of Ain Khudra, which lies along the course of the Wadi of Ain Khudra, is distinguished by the great abundance of water. The rocks that form much of the wadi are marly limestone, which take on a brilliant white hue in certain points, and sandstone.

113 bottom Badly eroded sandstone that shows all the marks of the elements is the prevailing geological form in this stretch of the Wadi Khudra, which is called Wadi Disco by the Beduins, since the arrangement of the rocks forms a sort of natural shelter, often used for evening entertainments and parties.

COLORED CANYON

Taking the paved road the leads from Nuweiba to the Tunnel Ahmed Hamdi, via Nakhl, fifteen kilometers, or ten miles, past the fork in the road, one will see on the right a grove of palm trees and a few Bedouin huts: this is the beginning of the oasis of Ain Furtaga. From here, on the right, a track begins that runs through the Wadi Nekheil, and winds up at the renowned Colored Canyon. The track is well marked, and can be driven by non-four-wheel drive vehicles, though it is not always easy.

Itinerary

After entering the track of Wadi Nekheil, which climbs slightly, and after driving twelve kilometers (seven-and-a-half miles), one reaches a fork in the road where one should take the left-hand track and continue for another kilometer (just over half a mile) until one reaches a splendid point of view that overlooks a vast erosion valley, where one is forced to park one's car and continue on foot. From here, on foot, one climbs down along a very steep trail cut into the side of the scarp until one reaches the bottom of the valley; here one continues, keeping to one's right. The wadi becomes progressively narrower until it is a very tight passageway, in a few places no wide than a meter (a yard), running between two sandstone cliffs that tower up about fifty meters (one hundred sixty five feet). This is the well known Colored Canyon, so called because the sandstone walls that flank it feature remarkable hues and shades of color, ranging from white to yellow and all the shades imaginable of red; they are particularly reminiscent of the similar formations found at Petra in Jordan. The narrowest and most impressive section of the canyon is about seven hundred meters (twenty-three hundred feet) in length, and presents two passages that require considerable fitness (and perhaps a little boost) to get through. After making one's way through this section, one finds that the canyon widens a bit and then enters a broad wadi, where one should keep to one's right. One then reaches a rock cliff with a steep trail that one must climb in order to return to the highland. If one has a driver, it would be a good idea to have the car come pick one up. Otherwise, it is necessary to walk back two-and-a-half kilometers (one-and-a-half miles) to pick up one's car where it was left.

114 The spectacular landscape that surrounds the Colored Canyon is dominated by rocks of marine origins, limestone and sandstone, which all work together to give the mountains their distinctive, warm hues.

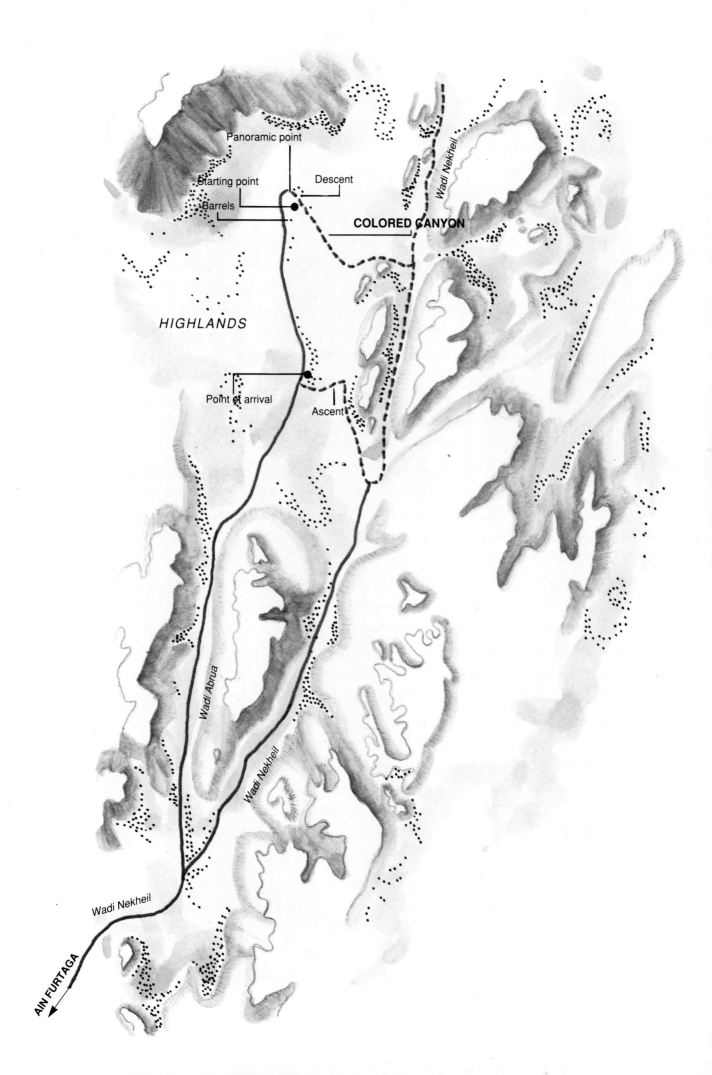

Panoramic point

Starting point

Descent

Barrels

COLORED CANYON

Wadi Nekheil

HIGHLANDS

Point of arrival

Ascent

Wadi Abrua

Wadi Nekheil

Wadi Nekheil

AIN FURTAGA

116 top left
The Colored Canyon
quickly narrows,
becoming a tight
tall cleft that in
certain points is
only a meter (or a
yard) across.

116 bottom left
The sheer and
exceedingly high
walls allow hikers
to see only a thin
blue strip of sky.

116 right
This picture gives us
a further example of
the unrivalled
charm that wafts
from the rocky walls
of the Colored
Canyon, upon
which nature has
playfully created an
exceedingly
spectacular vision.

117 left
The Colored Canyon takes its name from the rainbow hues of the sandstone into which it was carved by water erosion during the Quaternary Period. Similar formations are the setting of the renowned city of Petra in Jordan.

117 top right At the mouth of the canyon, which presents a few real challenges to hikers trying to follow its course, one must climb from the valley floor all the way up to the plateau; the final destination is a few kilometers from the point of departure, a distance which off-road vehicles can easily cover while the hikers work their way up the trail along the mountainside.

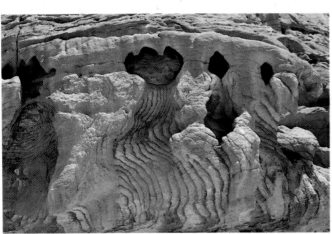

117 bottom right In the narrowest and most spectacular part of the Colored Canyon the walls rise to a considerable height, wedging in the deep fissure to points where it is no wider than a meter-and-a-half, or about five feet.

OASIS OF AIN UMM AHMED

Ain Umm Ahmed is one of the least visited and most beautiful oases in the Sinai. This is a huge palm grove broken here and there by small gardens and orchards cultivated by the few Beduin families that live in the nearby village. This is a place with abundant water, which springs forth pure and clear after long subterranean passages; gathered by the Beduins in the numerous cisterns partially concealed amidst the palm trees. Ain Umm Ahmed (the "Spring of the Mother of Ahmed") stretches along in Wadi El-Ain, and is slightly higher than the bed of the wadi; it is therefore safe from the terrible floods that sometimes occur in this area.

Itinerary
After passing through the oasis of Ain Furtaga, it is necessary to continue another twelve kilometers (seven-and-a-half miles) and pass through a checkpoint of the Egyptian army, where it will be necessary to show one's passport. After another six kilometers (about four miles), there is a track on the left that leads to the oasis of Ain Umm Ahmed. The track is well marked and can be easily recognized by the presence of a Beduin village, a few meters (yards) further along, on the left; the village consists of a few masonry houses near some handsome acacia trees. The track continues to climb, with a broad curve on the left, and then reaches a narrow passageway between huge boulders, and then continues onward with no further obstacles. After a few kilometers (miles) comes the most spectacular and scenic section of the route; the rocks are white and powdery at first, and then they take on all the colors imaginable, from light blue to ocher and deep red, in an array nuances that accompany the incredible surrounding lunar landscape. Especially worth noticing, is the majestic Ras el-Qelb (which means "Head of a Dog"), a mountain that stands some thousand meters (about 3,300 feet) high. The track then becomes a true road with a breccia surface that runs for a number of meters (yards) wedged between the mountain and the deep multicolored sandstone bed of a dry stream; finally one reaches the sandy Wadi el-Ain, dotted with acacias, palm trees, and wells protected by barbed wire. Then, a little further on, on the left, are the gardens of Ain Umm Ahmed and and on the right are the houses of the gardens' owners. From Ain Umm Ahmed the tracks continue along the Wadi Lethi and then Wadi Mikeimin and Wadi Khudra until Ain Khudra.

118 top Far less well known and less popular than Ain Khudra, the oasis of Ain Umm Ahmed is one of the loveliest in all of the Sinai. A watercourse runs its entire length, and around it stand impressive palm trees and acacias.

118 bottom The oasis of Ain Furtaga in the Wadi Watir is a major passage through which one must go in order to reach Ain Umm Ahmed.

*119 top The oasis of
Ain Umm Ahmed is
crossed by a small
stream that wends
amongst the
limestone rocks.*

*119 bottom
Perfectly
camouflaged amidst
the rock, a small
lizard keeps an eye
on intruders.*

SAINT CATHERINE

One can reach the highland of Saint Catherine by taking two different routes: the first cuts off from the road from Dahab to Nuweiba, the second runs from the road that skirts the Gulf of Suez and runs inland toward the center of the Sinai Peninsula along the great Wadi Feiran. Both of these roads converge near the tomb that is called the mausoleum of Sheikh Nabi Salah; Salah was a local saint and is revered as a prophet by the Beduins. The figure is not known to correspond to any clearly identified historical figure, and could well be a character taken from Biblical tradition From this point onward, the paved road runs along the Wadi el-Sheikh, which opens out into a highland that runs along a roughly northeast-southwest axis and then widens - near the tomb of Sheikh Harun - into the plain of el-Raha, meaning "the Plain of Rest." This plain is triangular in shape and its yellow sands contrast with the dark colors of the granitic mountains that surround it. In this plain, unfortunately now ruined beyond rescue by the construction of the Saint Catherine Tourist Village, the Hebrews camped and first laid eyes upon the Sacred Mountain (see Exodus 19, 1-2). Again, according to Biblical tradition, it was here that the famous Golden Calf was forged, and later shattered to bits by the wrath of Moses (see Exodus 19, 19-20). On the southern slope, two wadis open out and run parallel: Wadi el-Deir and Wadi el-Lega. At the westernmost point lies the plain of Melga where, in line with the town of Saint Catherine, the paved road comes to an end. Wadi el-Deir - or "Wadi of the Monastery," which is also known as Wadi Shoeib, meaning "Valley of the Horeb," or Wadi Jethro (after Moses's son-in-law) - begins near the small hill upon which is built the tomb of Sheikh Harun and the "Chapel of the Golden Calf." Further up the same hill is the monastery of Saint Catherine. The wadi is bounded by four mountainous groups: Gebel el-Deir, Gebel Moneiga, Gebel Musa, and Ras Safsafa. Gebel el-Deir, the eastern section of which is called

120 top Ras Safsafa, a name that in Arabic means the "peak of willows," is, with its three summits, one of the most distinctive mountains in the region of Saint Catherine. A paved road now runs through the Wadi Deir, coming within a few hundred meters or yards of the monastery of Saint Catherine.

120 center The plain of el-Raha, or "the plain of rest," is found in the Wadi el-Sheikh on a line with the mouth of the Wadi el-Deir: it was here that, according to tradition, the people of Israel halted to camp. The ancient caravan route, used by pilgrims and wayfarers until the nineteenth century to reach the monastery, crossed this broad sandy plain with a triangular shape, now disfigured by the construction of a huge tourist resort.

120 bottom At the mouth of the Wadi el-Deir, which leads to the monastery of Saint Catherine, on the summit of a small isolated hill, one can see two structures: this is the Mausoleum of the Sheikh Arun and the Chapel of the Golden Calf, built to commemorate the golden calf, made by Aaron for the Israelites while Moses was on Mount Sinai, receiving the Tablets of the Ten Commandments.

Gebel Megafa, marks the northern boundary of Wadi el-Deir. On its slopes, two chapels have been built (to the east and to the northeast of the monastery), dedicated to Saint Theodore and Saint Galatio. Alongside this mountain stands Gebel Moneiga, which is separated by a saddle from the imposing bulk of Gebel Musa. On the southwest side of Wadi el-Deir stands Ras Safsafa, or the "Peak of the Willows," which overlooks the plain of el-Raha and of Melga, and which culminates in three peaks: on the highest of these peaks stands a cross which was placed here to commemorate the fact that Moses on this spot

showed to the Hebrew people, gathered in the plain of el-Raha beneath, the tablets of the Ten Commandments (see Exodus 34, 29-35). The Wadi el-Lega opens out onto the plain of Melga and is separated from the Wadi el-Deir by Ras Safsafa. From here, a trail runs to Deir el-Ribwa, or "Monastery of the Twelve Apostles," and then on to Deir el-Arbain, or "Monastery of the Forty Martyrs," where the path begins that leads up to the summit of Gebel Katherina.

121 Just a few kilometers, or miles, from the monastery of Saint Catherine, near the intersection between Sheikh Nabi Sala with the road that runs down into the Wadi Feiran, there is a small cemetery and the mausoleum of Sheikh Nabi Sala, a holy man and a prophet who is greatly revered by

the Beduins of this region. We know of no specific historical basis for his identity; some believe that he was the founder of the Beduin tribe of the Sawalha, but this figure could also be a Biblical reminiscence persisting in the Beduin oral tradition, confusing this prophet with the prophet Moses.

Map labels:
Wadi Talah
Plain of el-Raha
Sheikh Harun
Wadi Sheikh
Gebel Ribsha
Gebel el-Deir
Plain of Melga
Wadi el-Deir
Deir el-Rahab
Gebel Megafa
Gebel el-Rahab
Ras Safsafa
Pass of Abu Gifa
Monastery St. Catherine
Wadi Zawatin
Wadi Tubuq
Wadi Jibal
Wadi el-Lega
Deir el-Arbain
Gebel Musa
Gebel Monega
Bir Shennar
Gebel Katherina
Observation Point
Gebel Zebir

PRACTICAL INFORMATION

At the intersection with the road that runs from Feiran and with the road that links Dahab and Nuweiba with the village Saint Catherine, there is a gas station and a rest-house called the Green Lodge. The Green Lodge, which offers rough but comfortable lodgings, can be considered an excellent point of departure for the many hikes and excursions that can be made in this area: the tour of the Monastery of Saint Catherine, the climb to the top of Gebel Musa, the climb to the top of Gebel Katherina, and the Blue Desert. Otherwise, one can stay at the Saint Catherine Village, where one stays in bungalows that are more comfortable than the lodging at the Green Lodge (although there is not half of the agreeable

atmosphere), or else in the guest house of the monastery itself, where it is possible to spend the night in an eminently dignified manner. In order to organize excursions, rent camels, and find a Beduin guide, one must rely upon the only specialized "agency" in the region: the Sheikh Musa Travel Mountain, which can be found in the village of Saint Catherine. It is worth knowing that the locals always tend to expand the time of the outings exaggeratedly, and it is extremely important to tell them exactly what you want to see, make a clear agreement in advance on how much is to be paid and how long the outing is to last. For the hike up Gebel Musa and the tour of the Blue Desert, a guide is completely unnecessary.

THE MONASTERY

122 The monastery
of Saint Catherine
stands at the foot of
Mount Moses, at an
altitude of 1,570
meters (5,149 feet)
above sea level. The
Byzantine emperor
Justinian founded
the monastery,

*122 The monastery
of Saint Catherine
stands at the foot of
Mount Moses, at an
altitude of 1,570
meters (5,149 feet)
above sea level. The
Byzantine emperor
Justinian founded
the monastery,*

*incorporating a
little church that
Constantine's
mother, Saint
Helena, had built in
A.D. 330 on the site
where, according to
tradition, Moses
saw the Burning
Bush*

The monastery of Saint Catherine is located in a valley at the foot of the Gebel Musa, at an elevation of 1,570 meters (5,150 feet) above sea level; it was founded by the Byzantine emperor Justinian between A.D. 527 and 547. Surrounded by a massive enclosure wall dating from the time of Justinian, the monastery was enlarged in a number of different phases of construction over the subsequent periods. The enclosure wall is of a wide range of heights and thicknesses because of the need to adapt it to configuration of the mountain; each side, therefore, has a length that varies from seventy to eighty meters (two hundred thirty to two hundred sixty two feet), a height that ranges from nine to eighteen meters (thirty to sixty feet), and a thickness of between 1.8 and 2.7 meters (six to nine feet). The wall that constitutes the north side is known as Diwar Duawara, or the "Wall of the Precipice"; it was rebuilt in 1312 and restored in 1800 at Napoleon's orders under the supervision of General Jean-Baptiste Kleber, who also built a corner watchtower, a square tower, and a central bastion with two more towers.

Fifteen centuries of history

In the Bible story, the Hebrews, after fifty days of marching through the mountains and the desert of the Sinai, reached the plain of el-Raha, where Moses received the Tablets of the Ten Commandments upon which Hebrew and Christian doctrines are founded. Mount Horeb, which in time came to be called Gebel Musa ("Mountain of Moses"), became the Holy Mountain by definition, a place of pilgrimage and prayer for the earliest Christians, a place around which small monastic communities sprang up quickly, but it was not until A.D. 330 that Helena, the mother of the Emperor Constantine - who had definitively put an end to the persecution of Christians with his famous edict of A.D. 313, ensuring freedom of worship for all - ordered the construction of a small church in the place which was said to be the site of the Burning Bush. The monastic community that lived around Gebel Musa continue to develop and grow over the subsequent centuries, and became the object of pilgrimages and veneration. Subsequently, Justinian ordered in A.D. 527 the construction of a full-fledged monastery with a great basilica, protected by an imposing enclosure wall that also contained the original church of Saint Helena, to defend the anchorites from Beduin raids. The basilica was subsequently decorated with the splendid mosaic which can still be seen,

known as the mosaic of the Transfiguration, hence the name of "Basilica of the Transfiguration."

This name however did not remain the church's definitive one, because successively - between the eighth and the ninth centuries - the monks found the body of Saint Catherine which, according to tradition, had been transported by angels to the summit of Gebel Katherina, but which had then disappeared. The body of the saint - or what was believed to be the body of the saint - was thereupon placed in a sarcophagus inside the basilica, where it still lies, and from then on the monastery was known as the Monastery of Saint Catherine. Despite the conquest of the Sinai Peninsual by Muslim Arabs in A.D. 641, the monks continued to live in the convent practically undisturbed, under the protection of a decree issued by Mohammed himself, ensuring their safety.

The volume of pilgrims declined markedly, and did not increase again until the eleventh century, during the Crusades.

Indeed, it was the Crusaders who spread throughout Europe the legend and cult of Saint Catherine, and the monastery in the Sinai became one of the great destinations for Christian pilgrimages, ranking up there with Jerusalem and Rome.

Even after the conquest of Egypt and the Sinai by the Ottoman sultans, the monastery was given protection under the new conquerors, with a decree issued by the sultan Selim I in 1517. The importance and the influence of the monastery continued to grow then even during this difficult period, and not only were subsidiary structures founded in Egypt and Palestine, but also on Crete, in Romania, and even in Russia. Napoleon too during his campaign in Egypt promulgated a decree protecting the monastery, which is still preserved in the Gallery of Icons; the French emperor also gave an order to help restore damaged sections of the enclosure wall.

123 top
The enclosure walls, which date from the time of the Emperor Justinian, surround and protect the numerous buildings that make up the monastery complex; these walls were restored again at the time of the expedition of Napoleon Bonaparte in Egypt. The central bastion, framed by two towers, and the tower at the northeastern corner, were in fact built by General Jean-Baptiste Kléber in 1801.

123 center One of the Beduins that serve in the monastery: these are the Djebelieh, or mountain Beduins, who are the descendants of a group of familes who were transported here from Bosnia and Wallachia during the reign of Justinian to serve the monks.

123 bottom
The majestic mountains of the Sinai seem to cluster protectively around the monastery of Saint Catherine.

124-125 The powerful enclosure walls that surround the monastery were built of local red granite; the height ranges from nine to fifteen meters (thirty to fifty feet), while the thickness in certain points is more than two meters (six-and-a-half feet).

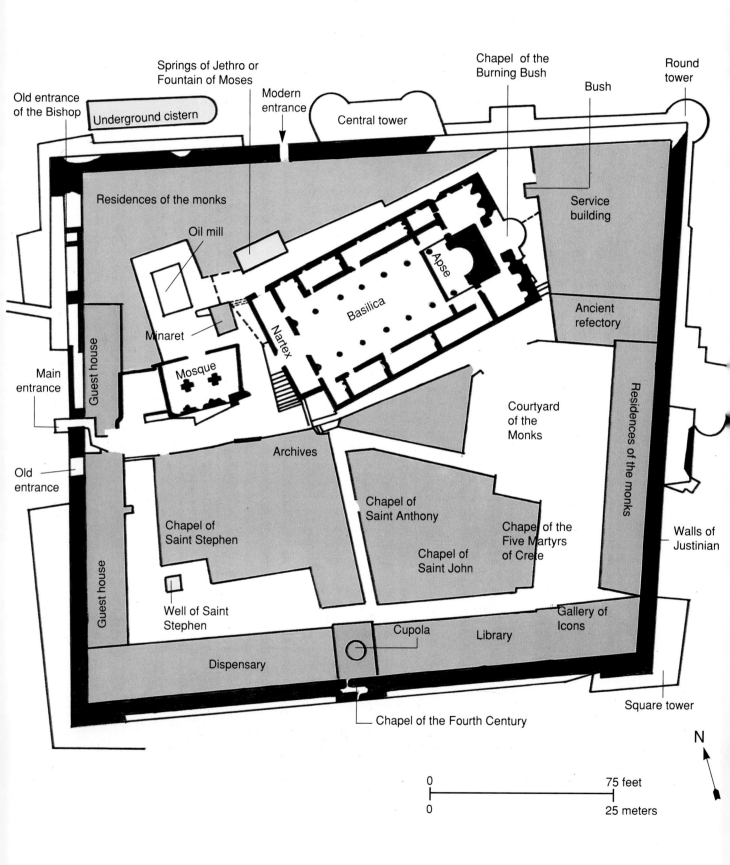

Old entrance
of the Bishop

Springs of Jethro or
Fountain of Moses

Underground cistern

Modern
entrance

Central tower

Chapel of the
Burning Bush

Bush

Round
tower

Residences of the monks

Oil mill

Service
building

Minaret

Narthex

Basilica

Apse

Ancient
refectory

Main
entrance

Guest house

Mosque

Old
entrance

Archives

Courtyard
of the
Monks

Residences of the monks

Chapel of
Saint Anthony

Chapel of the
Five Martyrs
of Crete

Walls of
Justinian

Chapel of
Saint Stephen

Chapel of
Saint John

Guest house

Well of Saint
Stephen

Cupola

Library

Gallery of
Icons

Dispensary

Chapel of the Fourth Century

Square tower

N

| 0 | 75 feet |
| 0 | 25 meters |

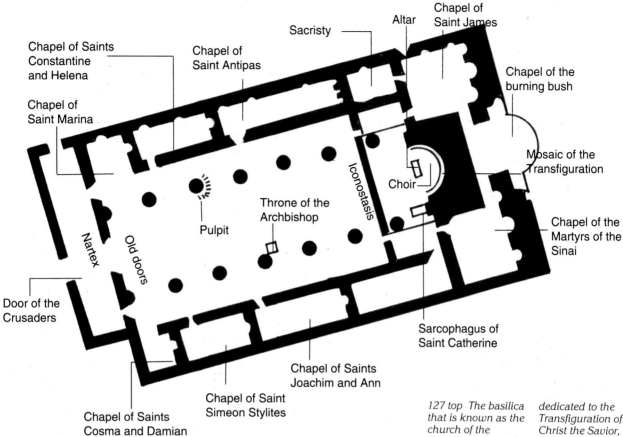

Chapel of Saints Constantine and Helena

Chapel of Saint Antipas

Sacristy

Altar

Chapel of Saint James

Chapel of the burning bush

Chapel of Saint Marina

Mosaic of the Transfiguration

Iconostasis

Choir

Throne of the Archbishop

Pulpit

Nartex

Old doors

Chapel of the Martyrs of the Sinai

Door of the Crusaders

Sarcophagus of Saint Catherine

Chapel of Saints Joachim and Ann

Chapel of Saint Simeon Stylites

Chapel of Saints Cosma and Damian

127 top The basilica that is known as the church of the Transfiguration is the most important building in the monastery; it has a three-aisle structure. Originally, in fact, the monastery was dedicated to the Transfiguration of Christ the Savior, and only later was it dedicated to Saint Catherine, a young marty of Alexandria. The basilica's bell tower was not built until 1871.

127 bottom Here we see an outline of the mosaic of the Transfiguration of Christ which adorns the vault of the sanctuary of the chief temple. Dating from the sixth century, it has survived to modern times in perfect condition. At the center of the image is Christ Transfigured, while to his right is Moses, and on his left, Elijah; at his feet are the apostles Peter, James, and John.

128 *top and center*
*On the interior of
the enclosure wall
are a number of
buildings, among
which we mention
the famous library,
the museum,
and the gallery of
icons, the refectory,
and the residences
of the monks. None
of these structures
can be toured, and
indeed only a minor
section of the
monastery can be
visited by tourists.*

*128 bottom
The central bastion,
and the corner
tower and the
square tower, were
built by General
Jean-Baptiste
Kléber in 1800, at
the orders of
Napoleon.*

The architecture of the monastery

The original entrance to the monastery was on the western side, while the modern-day entrance is on the northern side. After penetrating, therefore, into the monastery through the northern entrance, one will see on the left the fountain of Moses, also known as the well of Jethro where, according to the Bible, Moses - arriving in this valley after being expelled from Egypt - saved the seven daughters of Jethro from the rudeness of the shepherds; Jethro was the priest of an ancient local deity, and in a sign of gratitude, he gave one of his daughters to Moses as a wife (see Exodus, 2, 16-22).

This spring is the main source of fresh water for the convent, and its water is channeled through an underground basin situated before the northern wall of the monastery. After passing the

fountain of Moses, one finds oneself before a Byzantine-style three-nave basilica, built in A.D. 527. In front of the basilica is a narthex (a term used to indicate a vestibule or porch before the facade of the paleo-Christian basilicas, reserved for women, penitents, and catechumens), and the narthex has a wooden door dating from the eleventh century. On this door is written in Greek the words, "This is the Door of the Lord, the just can enter here."
In the narthex, a number of very fine icons are on display, the only ones that can be seen by the public. This is the entrance to the basilica, through a wooden four-part door dating from the sixth century: the abundance and wealth of the furnishings, the countless lamps hanging from the gilded ceiling, cannot help but surprise and impress the visitors. The basilica has a three-nave structure, which are separated by twelve columns, and it is adorned - among other things - by a magnificent iconostasis dating from the seventeenth century, the work of a Cretan monk named Jeremiah the Sinaite, depicting Christ, the Virgin Mary, Saint Catherine, Saint

Nicholas, Saint Michael, Saint John the Baptist, and the major liturgical feasts. At the end, above the choir and partially hidden by the countless lamps, is the celebrated Mosaic of the Transfiguration, with a great image of Christ in the center, surrounded by Moses, Elijah, and a number of apostles. To the right of the choir is a marble sarcophagus which is believed to contain the body of Saint Catherine. On the interior of the enclosure wall, there are many important structures, beside the basilica:

1) the bell tower, which was built in 1871, under the supervision of a monk named Basil. The nine bells, which are rung only for major liturgical functions, and never for daily functions, were donated by the Czar of Russia.

2) the "Chapel of the Burning Bush," adjacent to the church and built upon the spot where Moses saw the bush that burned but was not consumed (see Exodus, 3,5; 3, 1-12). The altar of the chapel, dedicated to the Annunciation of the Virgin, is believed to have been built upon the roots of the sacred bush; the apse is adorned with a mosaic dating from the sixth century, the period in which the bush is said to have been transported outside the apse.

3) the refectory, which is made up of a rectangular room with an arched vault and a rectangular wooden table brought here from Corfu in the eighteenth century. On the walls of this room are inscriptions left behind by pilgrims in the fifteenth century, who used this room as a dormitory.

4) the mosque, built in 1106 by transforming a chapel dedicated to St Basil, into an Islamic religious structure. Inside the mosque is a wooden *minbar*, an Arabic word which is used to indicate the pulpit from which the sermon is preached to the faithful on Friday, the only surviving example of a *minbar* dating from the Fatimid era. Adjacent to the mosque is a minaret that stands alongside the belltower of the basilica.

129 On the interior of the monastery of Saint Catherine, stand a number of construction one alongside another, in a haphazard juxtaposition of styles and architectural shapes; nonetheless this apparent disorder does absolutely nothing to jostle the meditative atmosphere of the place.

5) the library, which is considered to have the second finest collection of manuscripts (three thousand of them) and miniatures in the world, after the library of the Museums of the Vatican; unfortunately it is virtually impossible to gain access. These priceless codices, for the most part written in Greek, were produced (copied or written) by the monks themselves; this distinguishes the collection, making it unique. It was here that the German scholar Friedrich von Tischendorf discovered in 1844 the celebrated *Codex Sinaiticus*, which contained a fourth-century version of the Bible. This codex, which was made up of one hundred twenty-nine sheets of parchment, was donated to the Czar of Russia Alexander II in 1859, but in 1933 the Bolshevik government sold it to the British Museum, where it remains today. Adjacent to the library is the Gallery of Icons, which contains more than two thousand icons, many of them dating from the period between the

tenth and the fifteenth centuries, although there are a few that are even older. The icons were painted by the monks of the convent, who developed a "Sinaitic school of art" in their own right. Alongside the library there is also a treasury, including chalices, icons, candelabra, and other objects donated through the generosity of the faithful.

Adjacent to the monastery and outside of the enclosure wall are:

1) a garden, surrounded by tall cypresses, a true mountain oasis, with olive trees, fruit trees, and an orchard;

2) a cemetery, situated right in the middle of the garden.
For lack of space, the remains of the monks are reexhumed after a certain period of time has passed, and placed in the nearby crypt of the chapel of Saint Tryphon, which has been turned into an ossuary, called the Charnel House.

130 top right
A low wall surrounds the site where, according to tradition, Moses saw the Burning Bush.

130 bottom right
Polychromatic decorative elements embellish the facade of the chapel of Saint John Theologus.

130 top left
At the center of the picture, we can see the Basilica of the Transfiguration, a sacred building that contains precious works of art, in particular, many icons.

130 bottom left
Near the "Wells of Moses," one can admire a remarkable arch dating from the reign of Justinian.

131 top left
This picture shows one of the crosses carved into the exterior stones of the enclosure wall of the monastery.

131 right At the entrance of the Basilica of the Transfiguration, we find a remarkable door made of carved wood, dating from the twelfth century, which leads to the narthex.

131 bottom left
On the interior of the monastery is the "Well of Moses," one of the principal sources of spring water for the convent. According to the Bible, Moses met the daughters of Jethro on this site, and the eldest of them later became his wife.

132-133
The interior of the basilica, which is lavishly adorned with countless lamps that hang from the ceiling, is dominated by the huge wooden iconostasis dating from the seventeenth century, decorated with depictions of Christ, the Virgin Mary, and a number of saints, including Saint Catherine.

134 The Gallery of the Icons contains more than two thousand icons, all of them the creations of monks in the convent, for the most part work dating from the tenth to fifteenth centuries; among the most exquisite and precision is the celebrated "Scala per il cielo," by Saint John Climaco, a Sinaitic monk who lived in the seventh century.

135 The icons of the monastery of Saint Catherine are painted on wood, and are the product of a sophisticated and original school of art.

135

*136 top
The monastery complex of Saint Catherine stands at the end of the Wadi el-Deir, a place-name that means "the valley of the monastery"; the complex includes a number of features that lie without the enclosure walls dating from the time of Justinian, such as the dormitory, the ossuary, the orchard, and the gardens.*

*136 bottom
The gardens of the monastery are shaded by tall cypress trees, many olive trees, and a great many fruit trees.*

The monks of Saint Catherine

The monks of Saint Catherine have an independent and autonomous structure, at the head of which is an archbishop, who performs his functions and duties, with the assistance of a council. The monastic order of the Sinai, to which the monks belong, originally belonged to the Church of Rome, and was recognized officially in 1260 by Pope Innocent IV, but two centuries later, in 1439 - at the time of the Council of Florence - the monastery broke away in order to follow the liturgy of the Eastern Orthodox Church. The monks follow the rule of Saint Basil, which calls for one to rise at 2:30 in the morning, for prayer and the celebration of the liturgy from 4 to 7:30, with Vespers and the associated functions from 3 in the afternoon until 5.

After Vespers, the monks would gather for the only meal of the day, a frugal feast to be sure. The Order of Saint Catherine adopted Greek as the language of all liturgical functions, and most of the monks themselves are Greek. The monks, who now number only about fifteen, were far more numerous in ancient times (as many as three or four hundred in the years between the tenth and fourteenth centuries); they are still assisted in their day-to-day routines by Muslim Beduin servants from the tribe of Djebelieh (meaning, "those of the mountain"). These tribesmen are the descendents of a group of some two hundred families originally from Wallachia and the region around Alexandria, and were transported at the orders of Justinian for the purpose of serving the monastery; they later converted to Islam.

PRACTICAL INFORMATION

A tour of the monastery is often - and mistakenly - considered to be one of the essential moments of any trip to the Sinai. Although this is certainly true of the area around the monastery - not to be missed - it is worth keeping in mind that the tour of the interior may prove to be a letdown, because most of the buildings are off limit to tourists. Tourists are excluded from the library and the Chapel of the Burning Bush; they are allowed to see the church, the fountain of Moses, the shrub that is said to be the Burning Bush, and the ossuary. Moreover, one is allowed to tour the monastery only in the morning hours (from 9 am until noon), which is closed on Friday, Sunday, major religious holidays, and during certain periods of spiritual retirement. It is a good idea, therefore, to inquire with agencies or even to telephone ahead directly to the monastery before setting off.

137 top Not far from the monastery is a small chapel, surrounded by a low stone wall.

*137 center and bottom left
The monastery today is populated by about fifteen monks, most of them of Greek descent, who faithfully adhere to the liturgy of the Eastern Orthodox Church, and the rule of Saint Basil. The monastery is an autonomous structure headed by an archbishop, who governs jointly with a council.*

*137 bottom right
In the garden of the monastery, in the crypt of the chapel of Saint Trifonio, is the ossuary where the mortal remains of generations of monks are preserved.*

137

GEBEL MUSA

The climb up Gebel Musa - ("the Mountain of Moses"), believed to be the same as Mount Horeb, from the Bible - is an excursion not to be missed by any of those who go to tour the site of Saint Catherine. The hike to the summit (2,286 meters, or 7,498 feet) requires about three hours' time, and be made by two different routes, which both converge along the final part of the hike. The first route - called *Sikket Saydna Musa*, or "The Path of Moses" - is traditionally said to have been walked first by Moses when he climbed the mount; it consists of a long steep stairway cut directly into the living rock by the monks. This stairway has some thirty-seven hundred stairs, and begins in one of two ways: either with a track that climbs up parallel with the southern side of the monastery walls, or else with a track that splits off from the central wadi track, in a line with the two small stone buildings that one leaves behind on the left. After a climb of about thirty minutes, one passes the "Spring of Moses" which gurgles out into a small grotto and then runs past a chapel dedicated to the Virgin Mary. After passing this point, one next encounters the Gate of

Confession - so called because there was once in ancient times a monk who heard confession here from pilgrims, in order that they might accede to the summit of the sacred mountain cleansed of their sins - and the Gate of Saint Stephen. This takes one - after climbing three thousand steps - to a handsome plain surrounded by granite mountains, known as the "Amphitheater of the Seventy Wise Man of Israel," inasmuch as the Seventy Wise Men who accompanied Moses on his climb stopped here, because only the prophet himself could present himself to the presence of God (see Exodus 24,1-11). In this natural amphitheater, shaded by great cypresses and by an olive tree, one finds a spring and the hermitage of Saint Stephen, while on a summit that lies southward, there are two chapels dedicated to Moses and the Prophet Elijah. From here, another track starts out, leading one to the summit of Ras Safsafa, after passing a number of chapels dedicated to Saint John the Baptist, Saint Ann, Saint Joachin, and the Virgin Mary. After climbing the northeast wall of the amphitheater, one reaches the intersection with the second route: this is the starting

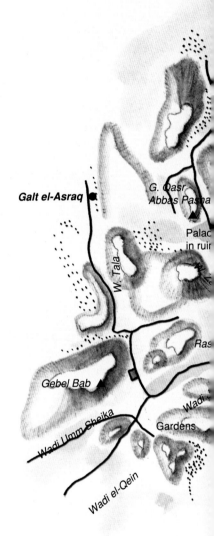

138 A small clearing in the shadow of the mountains, situated at the end of the first section of the stairway that runs from the monastery to the Mountain of Moses, is called the "amphitheater of the Seventy Wise Men of Israel": it is believed that the elders who were accompanying Moses were forced to halt to watch from afar the power of God, while the prophet Moses alone was allowed to continue to the summit of the mount.

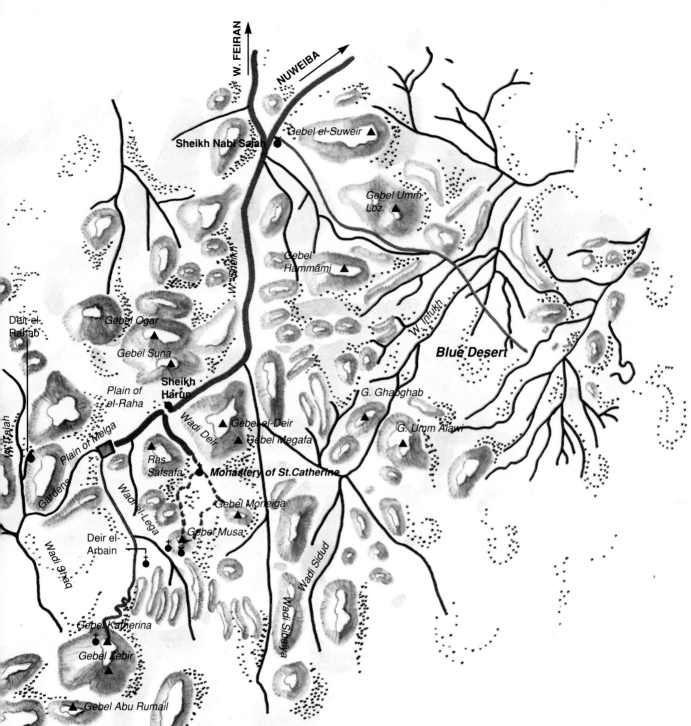

The map shows various locations in the Sinai region including:

W. FEIRAN
NUWEIBA
Gebel el-Suweir ▲
Sheikh Nabi Salah ●
Gebel Umm Loz ▲
Gebel Hammâmi ▲
Deir el-Rahab
Gebel Ogar ▲
Gebel Suna ▲
Sheikh Harun
Plain of el-Raha
W. Itlah
Plain of Melga
Ras Safsafa
Gardens
Wadi el-Lega
Deir el-Arbain
Wadi Shaq
Gebel Katherina
Gebel Zebir ▲
Gebel Abu Rumail ▲
Wadi Deir
Gebel el-Deir ▲
Gebel Megafa ▲
Monastery of St.Catherine ●
Gebel Moneiga ▲
Gebel Musa
Wadi Sidud
Wadi Sibaiya
G. Ghabghab ▲
G. Umm Alawi ▲
Blue Desert
W. Intukh
W. Sheikh

point of the last stairway (seven hundred steps), which leads to the summit of Gebel Musa. Along this stairway, at roughly the halfway point, one can encounter an odd shape cut into the granite by the force of erosion. The shape is reminiscent of a camel's pawprint. The Beduins call this *Athar Nagat el-Nabi*, which means "Pawprint of the She-Camel of the Prophet," although it is not certain which prophet is indicated by this oral tradition. On the summit of Gebel Musa, another chapel dedicated to the Holy Trinity was built on the site where, according to tradition, God appeared in the form of a cloud of fire and spoke to Moses

(see Exodus 24,15-18). From here the view is spectacular, especially in the dawning light, and one's gaze ranges over all the surrounding mountains and - on clear days - as far as the Gulf of Eilat. The chapel, rebuilt in 1934 on the ruins of an existing church from the fourth or fifth century, is decorated inside with frescoes illustrating the life of Moses. Alongside the chapel, slightly to the west, is a small mosque that was built in the twelfth century. Beneath this mosque is supposedly the cave where Moses spent forty days and where the Lord appeared to the prophet Elijah (see Exodus 24,5-18;

Kings, 9, 8-13). The second route, which is longer but not as difficult, can accommodate camels for part of its length; it is called the *Sikket el-Basha*, or "Route of the Pasha," as it was built during the reign of the pasha Abbas I. The trail runs for about five hundred meters (1,640 feet) along the bed of the Wadi El-Deir, sandwiched between Gebel Musa and Gebel Moneiga, then it rises, twisting, along the slopes of Gebel Musa until it reaches a narrow passage that looms above the amphitheater of the Seventy Wise Men of Israel, where it hooks up with the first road.

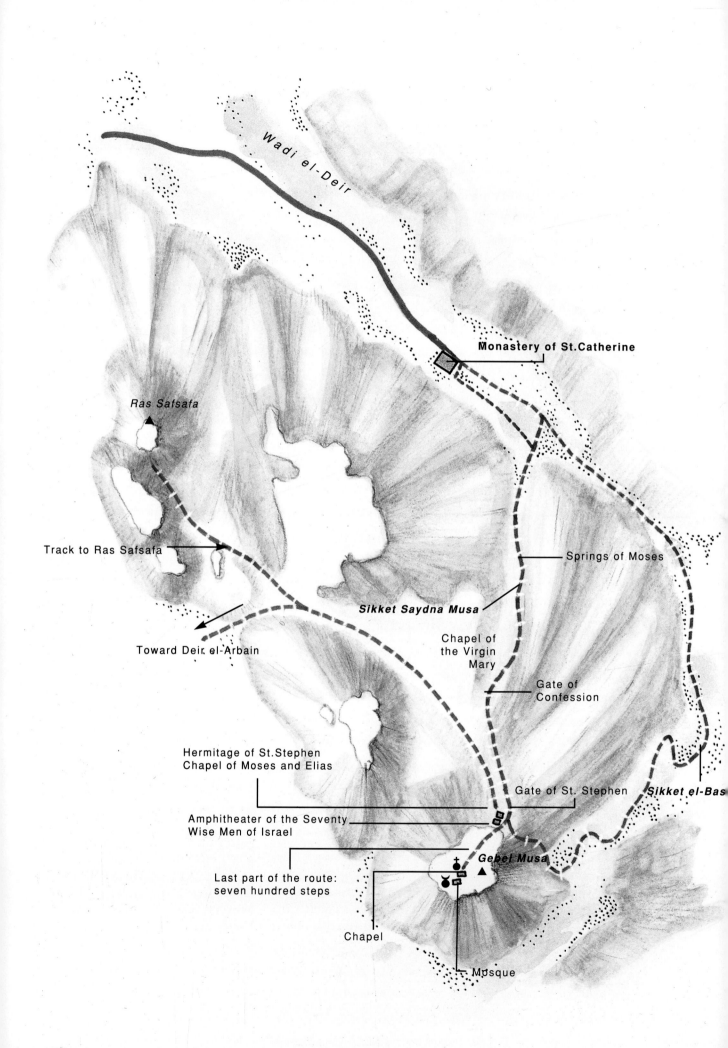

Wadi el-Deir

Monastery of St.Catherine

Ras Safsafa

Track to Ras Safsafa

Springs of Moses

Sikket Saydna Musa

Toward Deir el-Arbain

Chapel of
the Virgin
Mary

Gate of
Confession

Hermitage of St.Stephen
Chapel of Moses and Elias

Gate of St. Stephen

Sikket el-Bas

Amphitheater of the Seventy
Wise Men of Israel

Gebel Musa

Last part of the route:
seven hundred steps

Chapel

Mosque

It is traditional to set out on the hike to Gebel Musa at dawn in order to enjoy the spectacular vision of the first light of day setting the surrounding mountains aflame with contagious color. It is therefore necessary to set out at least three hours before dawn, equipped with electric flashlights, good mountain hiking boots and heavy garments because the temperature on the summit falls sharply, and often wind tears away what warmth is left. It is best to know in advance that the spectacular colors of dawn are however often ruined by the vast numbers of people who make this climb. Moreover, upon reaching the chapel on the summit of the mountain, is difficult even to find a way through the sleeping bags who sleep on the mountain top, and amidst the mountains of offal left by this human fauna. Generally, one climbs up (on foot or by camel), following *Sikket el-Basha* on the way up and coming down by *Sikket Saydna Musa*. There are a number of refreshment stands along the route.

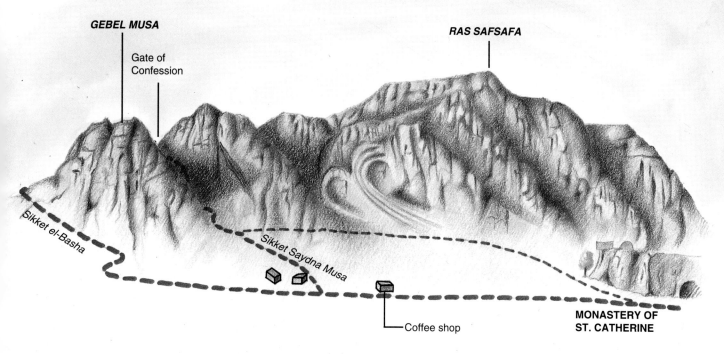

GEBEL MUSA

Gate of Confession

RAS SAFSAFA

Sikket el-Basha

Sikket Saydna Musa

Coffee shop

MONASTERY OF ST. CATHERINE

141 top A steep stairway with 3,700 steps leads up to the Gate of Confession: in accordance with tradition, a monk would wait here to receive the confessions of the many pilgrims, who could — thus cleansed of sin — then continue on to the holiest part of the mountain.

141 bottom The summit of the Mountain of Moses is occupied by a small mosque and a chapel dedicated to the Holy Trinity, built in 1934 on the ruins of a previously existing religious structure. Tradition has it that on this spot God spoke to Moses.

142-143 From the summit of the Mountain of Moses, rising some 2,285 meters, or 7,495 feet, above sea level, one can admire a spectacular vista of the surrounding mountains.

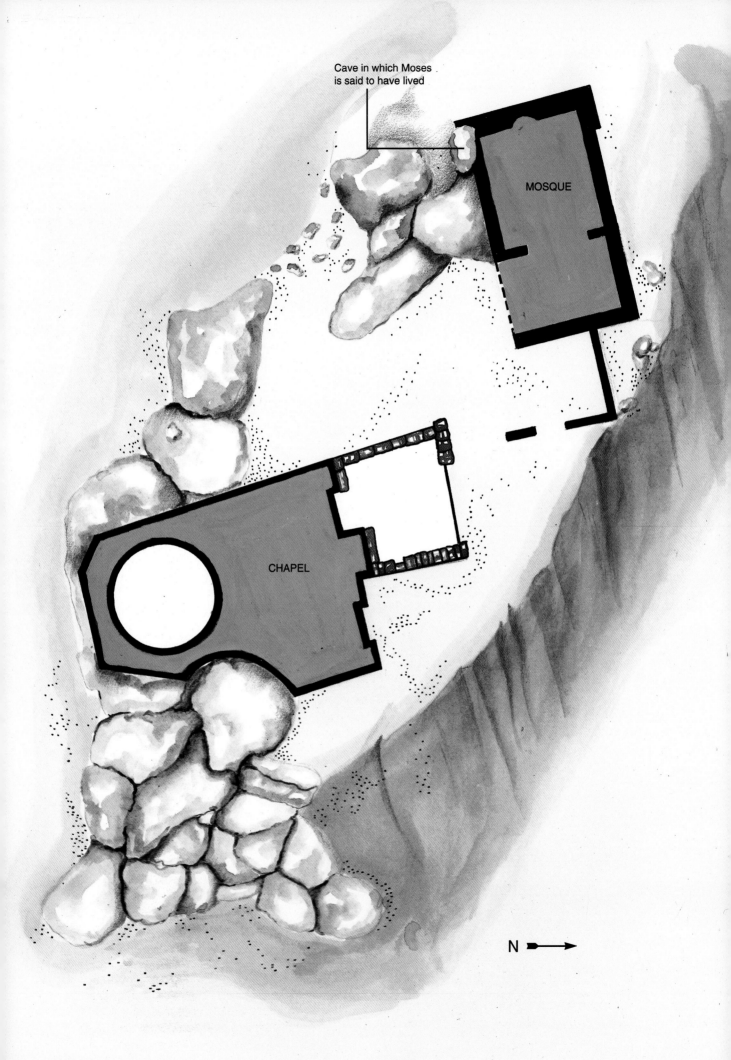

Cave in which Moses
is said to have lived

MOSQUE

CHAPEL

N ➡

145 top The little chapel atop the Mountain of Moses, seen by the faint light of dawn.

145 center The chapel of the Holy Trinity was built in 1933 upon the ruins of a temple dating from the time of Justinian.

145 bottom It takes some three hours of hard hiking to reach the summit of the imposing granite bulwark of the Mountain of Moses.

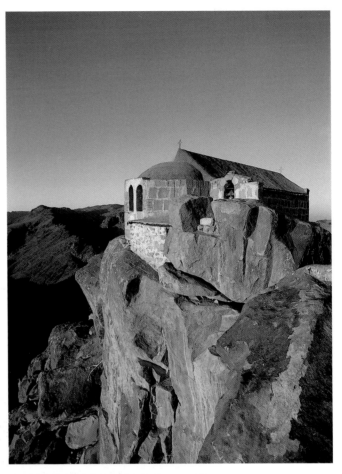

VILLAGE OF SAINT CATHERINE GALT EL-AZRAQ

All of the excursions heading for the mountains to the southwest of the village of Saint Catherine set out from Wadi Abu Gifa.

By following a well-marked path that often consists of steps cut neatly into the living rock and which climbs at a zigzag through the gardens and huts of the Beduins, one comes to the Pass of Abu Gifa. Off to one's left, one can see Deir el-Ribwa, more like a modern home in the mountains than like anything one thinks of as a monastery. Off to the right, on the other hand, one can see a trail that wends its way up a high mountain called Gebel Seru or Gebel Rahab by the Arabs. This trail, used routinely by the locals to lead their flocks to graze, runs through a pass and then descends steeply down the other side of the mountain, leading finally to Deir el-Rahab (into which no visitors or tourists are admitted), tucked away in a deep valley abounding in fresh-water springs, handsome gardens, and cypresses.

After going over the Pass of Abu Gifa, one climbs down a steep slope that culminates in the head of Wadi Tubuq. From here, on the right, is the narrow mouth of the Wadi Talah which, with a path drawn along the bed of a stream that wanders amidst the maze of enormous granite boulders, also leads to Deir el-Rahab.

If, on the other hand, one continues southwest along the bed of Wadi Tubuq, amidst handsome gardens and flourishing pomegranate shrubs, apple trees, almond trees, and olive trees, and then one passes the mouth of the Wadi Shaq, which opens out on one's left (a walk of one hour twenty minutes from the beginning of the hike). After passing through a narrow ravine with granite walls, the wadi heads determinedly in a west-southwesterly direction. From this point one can enjoy a magnificent view of Gebel Katherina, which rises in all its glory to the southeast.

From here, one continues along into the southern section of the

Wadi Zawatin. On one's right, a short trail leads to a stone hut that is often used by Beduins and by other tourists as a shelter for the night. A few hundred meters (yards) further along, one sees a branch of the same Wadi Zawatin, known as Nabq Zawatin, in line with a dense grove of olive trees.

If, on the other hand, one chooses to proceed directly along Wadi Zawatin in a northwesterly direction, then one will arrive at Gebel Abbas. After climbing back up Nabq Zawatin, one passes a small Beduin cemetery on one's left, and then one enters the broad plain of the Wadi Jibal, which runs in a southwesterly direction.

The highland then narrows into a steep rocky downhill slope, that turns into a small stream in the winter. To one's right and left, there are a great many gardens and wells, and the track runs parallel to a long wall which is the boundary of Beduin lands.

At a distance of a three-and-a-half hours' walk from the beginning of the hike, one comes up with Gebel Misman, with its distinctive round top rising off to one's left. Immediately after one passes this mountain, one will note off to one's left a trail that leads to the splendid wells of Ain Naghila. Proceeding along the trail that runs down through the Wadi Jibal, one curves toward the northwest, amidst granite boulders with odd shapes. A short distance beyond, one encounters

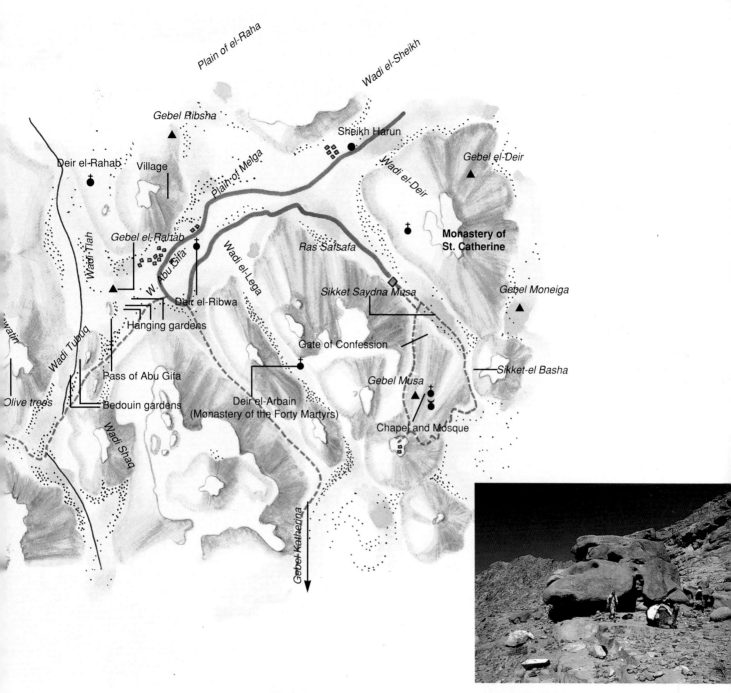

Plain of el-Raha

Wadi el-Sheikh

Gebel Ribsha

Sheikh Harun

Gebel el-Deir

Deir el-Rahab

Village

Plain of Melga

Wadi el-Deir

Wadi Tlah

Gebel el-Rahab

W. Abu Gifa

Wadi el-Lega

Ras Safsafa

Monastery of
St. Catherine

Deir el-Ribwa

Hanging gardens

Sikket Saydna Musa

Gebel Moneiga

Wadi Tubuq

Pass of Abu Gifa

Gate of Confession

Sikket-el Basha

watin

Olive trees

Bedouin gardens

Deir el-Arbain
(Monastery of the Forty Martyrs)

Gebel Musa

Wadi Shaq

Chapel and Mosque

Gebel Katherina

147 top In Farsh Rumanna, Behind this huge boulder is a small cavern used chiefly in the winter, when the weather is chilly and harsh, by Beduins and hikers forced to sleep outdoors.

147 bottom From the top of the pass of Abu Gifa, one can enjoy a magnificent view of the plains of Melga and el-Raha.

a village of drywall stone huts, which is called *Marufia* by the Beduins; here one may be able to find overnight accommodations. After passing these houses, the route follows the righthand bank of the wadi, which opens out into a broad plain, at the far end of which one reaches the site known as Farsh Rumanna (the "Plain of Pomegranates," a five-hours' walk from the trailhead). From this magnificent place abounding in water, one can start out on a number of different hikes, and sleep in stone houses with adequate if admittedly spartan furnishings. Toward the west, facing the houses, there is an opening amidst the rocks, marked by two poles; through here, one can reach a handsome plain where, alongside a number of more recent Beduin tombs, there are a number of sepulchers dating from the Bronze Age. The plain is bounded to the west by Gebel Nabq Baharia, where a steep downhill trail leads back to the wells of Ain Naghila. Setting out from Farsh Rhumanna, one climbs down along the streambed and along the wadi itself, which constitutes a continuation of Wadi Jibal; here it is called Wadi Talah, however. After just two hours of walking, one reaches a magnificent observation point from which one can view in the distance the dark silhouette of the imposing Gebel Tarbush and, further down, two deep valleys whose brilliant green water contrasts with the color of the surrounding rocks: the lower well is the renowned Galt el-Azraq, the "blue well." The very steep descent that leads down to the streambed takes no more than twenty minutes' time; one is then at the Galt, where the water of stream forms a splendid cascade. During the summer months, one can enjoy a splendid plunge into this small mountain lake basni, surprisingly deep (it drops down to seven meters, or about twenty-three feet).

148 top A steep little path that winds along the side of the mountain, running past a great many hanging gardens, allows one to reach the pass of Abu Gifa, and represents an obligatory route leading to the many mountain trails in the region of Saint Catherine.

148 center The Wadi Jibal is abundant in water and lush vegetation, and is dotted with small orderly gardens.

148 bottom The winding path that runs from Farsh Rumanna all the way to the deep basin known as Galt el-Azraq, passes through a rocky bank.

149 top At the mouth of the Wadi Jibal, one encounters a small Beduin cemetery.

149 center From Farsh Rumanna the route continues downhill, running alongside a little brook which ripples along the course of the Wadi Jibal; from this point forth, this wadi takes the name of Wadi Talah.

149 bottom The Galt el-Azraq, or "the blue well," is one of the most remarkable places in the mountains of Saint Catherine: the waters of the little stream, which form a diminutive waterfall, have dug out a basin some six or seven meters (about twenty feet) in depth, a delightful diving spot.

GEBEL KATHERINA

150 top In this picture we can recognize the eastern slope fo the Gebel Katherina; in the distance we can see the waters of the gulf of Suez.

150 bottom The Wadi el-Lega runs parallel to the Wadi el-Deir, the site of the monastery of Saint Catherine; it provides the easiest access route to the Gebel Katherina. At the furthermost point of the wadi is a convent called Deir el-Arbain, meaning the "Convent of the Forty Martyrs," built to commemorate forty monks killed by Beduins.

The climb up to Gebel Katherina is less assiduously used than that up to Gebel Musa, even though the view from the summit of this 2,642-meter-tall mountain (8,665-foot) is in all likelihood superior to that visible from the peak of Gebel Musa. In any case, here one is sure one will be alone. The trail that leads up starts on the plain of Melga and then follows the bed of the Wadi el-Lega, running parallel with the Wadi el-Deir. One can drive all the way up to the Convent of the Holy Apostles (Deir el-Ribwua), and then one must continue on foot, climbing the Wadi el-Lega. After about two kilometers (a mile-and-a-half), at the Convent of the Forty Martyrs (Deir el-Arbain), built to commemorate forty monks who were slaughtered by the Bedouin. From here on, the trail leaves the wadi-bed and runs up along its left slope. After climbing up through the gorge known as Shaqq Musa, one reaches a small flat area with a spring of fresh water. This is Bir el-Shenar, "the Well of the Patrialges," which stands at an altitude of 2,000 meters, or 6,560 feet. The trail runs twisting up the slope of the mountain, and finally one comes within sight of the summit, which is marked by a distinctive white chapel. After reaching the ridge, connecting Gebel Katherina with Gebel Zebir (2,644 meters, or 8,672 feet). Gebel Zebir is the tallest peak in the Sinai peninsula. Here a stairway begins which leads up to the chapel, where there are two small rooms in which one can take one's rest.
NB: The hike up Gebel Katherina will take about five hours to climb and three hours to descend.

PRACTICAL INFORMATION
In the headquarters of the Sheikh Musa Mountanial Travelling Office one can find a trekking itinerary made to order, with a Bedouin guide, a camel drover, and camels to suit the weight of the baggage to be loaded.
To give the reader a working idea, the cost of guide, drover, and two camels should run about one hundred fifteen Egyptian pounds a day, though it may be higher if the route chosen is a particularly tough one.

151 top From the Wadi Sheikh one enjoys a splendid view of Ras Safsafa.

151 center
The massive bulk of the Gebel Umm Shomer, and behind it, the Gebel Katherina, both seen from the east.

151 bottom
Running up the Wadi Zavatin and then taking the Wadi Shaq, which leads south, one will note in the distance the impressive dark bulk of the Gebel Katherina, the highest peak on the Sinai peninsula.

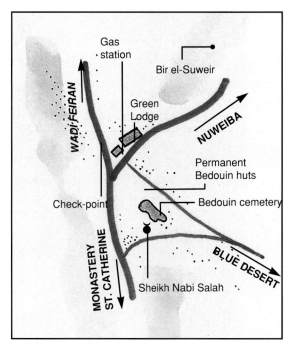

THE BLUE DESERT

With the name of "Blue Desert" one indicates a stretch of plateau that runs to the west of the mausoleum of Sheikh Nabi Salah where, over a surface area of fifteen square kilometers (nearly six square miles), a Belgian artist named Jean Verame - between 1980 and 1981, with permission from the late Anwar Sadat - painted a great many boulders here blue, the symbol of peace, to celebrate the end of the war between Egypt and Israel. Even though this very unusual artistic creation - which required the use of ten tons of paint - has caused a great deal of discussion, the "blue desert" remains the only place this author knows of where the unnatural color of the boulders, in glaring contrast with the ocher-yellow shades of the desert, give the rocks a remarkable plasticity, turning them into quasi-natural sculptures.

Itinerary
There is a well beaten track that will accommodate any type of vehicle, and it splits off from the paved road leading to the monastery of Saint Catherine, immediately after the intersection with a road leading from Feiran, and in line with the the mausoleum of Sheikh Nabi Salah. This road leads southeast. After travelling along it for six kilometers (four miles), one is in the area of the "Blue Desert ," which stretches over a distance of four kilometers (two-and-a-half miles). Most of the painted boulders can be seen off to the right of the track.

152 Between 1980 and 1981 a Belgian artist named Jean Verame painted these rocks and boulders a bright blue; they extend across an upland just a few kilometers (or miles) from the monastery of Saint Catherine.

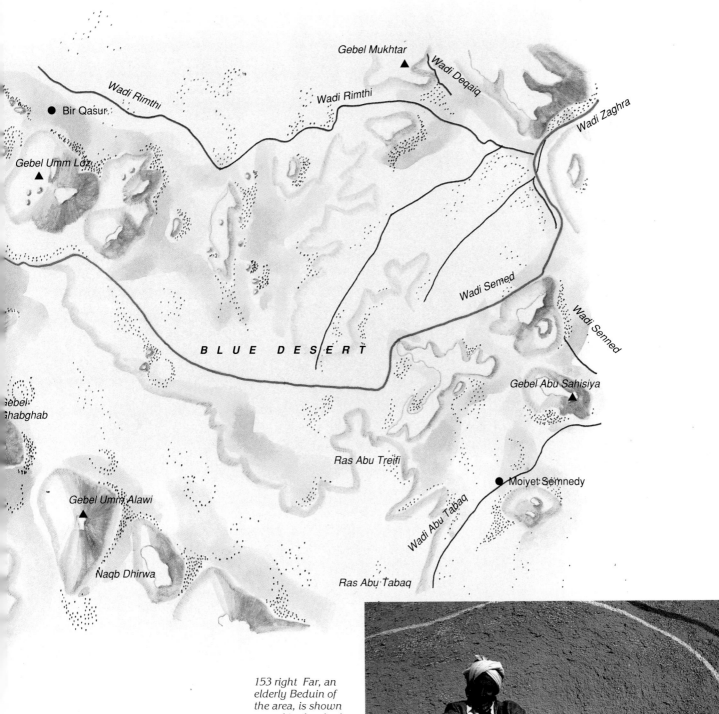

BLUE DESERT

Gebel Mukhtar

Wadi Deqaiq

Wadi Rimthi

Wadi Rimthi

Wadi Zaghra

● Bir Qasur

Gebel Umm Loz

Wadi Semed

Wadi Senned

Gebel Abu Sahisiya

Gebel Ghabghab

Ras Abu Treifi

● Moiyet Semnedy

Gebel Umm Alawi

Wadi Abu Tabaq

Naqb Dhirwa

Ras Abu Tabaq

153 left In order to complete his remarkable project, Jean Verame used ten tons of paint.

153 right Far, an elderly Beduin of the area, is shown seated in the shade of the largest of the blue boulders, selling magnificent quartz crystals and other minerals to passing tourists.

GLOSSARY

Transliteration and translation of the arabic word used in the text

Ain = spring
Bir = well
Chark = east
Darb = trail
Deir = convent
Fersh = plateau
Galt = body of water
Garb = west
Gebel = mount
Haggar = stone
Hamman = bath
Kebir = large

Khirberh = ruins
Kibla = south
Maghara = caves
Maghreb = west
Maiya = water
Marsa = bay
Naqub = pass
Nabi = prophet
Nebka = valley of small dunes
Qalaat = fortress
Qasr = castle
Ramleh = sand

Ras = headland, promontory, cape
Sahl = plain
Seih = stream
Seil = stream
Sheikh = chief
Shemal = north
Sidd = waterfall
Sikka = road
Tella = gorge
Wadi = valley
Umm = mother

USEFUL NUMBERS

HOTELS

SHARM EL-SHEIKH

Barracuda Can village (062)600442.
Cateract (062)600280/1 - fax (062)600282, *Naama Bay.*
Cliff Top Hotel (062)600251-4- fax (2)3922228, *Sharm el-Maya.*
Dolphin Hotel (062)600656.
El-Baraka Village (062)600378 - fax (062)600878.
El-Keheima Resort (062)600167/8 - fax (062)600166, *Sharm el-Maya.*
Gafy Land (062)600211/2 - fax 600210, *Naama Bay.*
Ghazala Hotel (062)600150/6 - fax 600155, *Naama Bay.*
Halomy Sharm Village (062)600681-9 - fax 600134, *Naama Bay.*
Helnan Marina Sharm (062)600170, *Naama Bay.*
Hilton Fayrouz (062)600141/2 - fax (2)770726, *Naama Bay.*
Hilton Residence (062)600267/6 - fax (2)770726, *Sharm el-Maya.*
Hotel Aquamarine, (062)600175/79 - fax (062)600177 *Naama Bay.*

Kanabesh Village (062)600184/6 - fax (062)600185, *Naama Bay.*
Layalina Cataract (062)600280 - fax (062)600282, *Naama Bay.*
LTI Seti Sharm (062)600870/7 - fax (062)600392, *Sharm el-Maya.*
Marina Sharm Hotel (062)600170/1, *Naama Bay.*
Mövenpick (062)600100/10 - fax (062)600111/5, *Naama Bay.*
New Tiran Hotel (062)600225 - fax (062)600220, *Naama Bay.*
Pigeon House (062)600995 - fax (062)600995, *Naama Bay.*
Safety Land (062)600359-600373, *Sharm el-Maya.*
Sanarif (062)600197/8 - fax (062)600196/5, *Naama Bay.*
Seti Hotel (062)600147, *Sharm el-Maya.*
Shark Bay (062)600942/3 - fax (062)600944, *Shark Bay.*
Sharm Club (Venta club) (062)600260/2 - fax (062)600263, *Tower Bay.*
Sheikh Coast (062)600835 - fax (062)600836, *Coral Bay.*

Sonesta (062)600725/6, *Naama Bay.*
Sonesta Beach Resort (062)600733, *Naama Bay.*
Tiran Village (062)600221 - fax (062)600166, *Naama Bay.*
Tower Hotel (062)600229 - fax (062)600220, *Tower Dive Site.*
Tropicana Hotel (062)600652 - fax (062)600649, *Naama Bay.*
Youth Center Sharm (062)600644, *Sharm el-Maya.*

DAHAB

Canyon Dive Site (062)640043, *Canyon Dive Site.*
Ganet Sinai Hotel (062)640440 - fax (062)640441.
PLM Azur (062)640301 - fax (2)776736.
INMO (062)640370/1 - fax (062)640371, *el-Mashraba.*
PLM Holiday Village (062)600403 - fax (062)600890.

NUWEIBA

Bawaki (062)500470, *Nuweiba-Taba.*
Baracuda Hotel (062)520300
Basata (2)3501829, *Ras Burqa.*
Dolphin Beach Hotel (2)771932, *Nuweiba-Taba.*

El-Salam Village (062)500440
El-Waha (062)500420/1.
Hilton Coral Beach (062)520320.
Nuweiba Holiday Village, (062)500402.
Sally Land (062)530380, *Nuweiba-Taba.*
Sayadin Beach Hotel (062)500340 - fax (062)520340/1.

TABA

Taba Hilton (062)763136 - fax (2)747044, *Taba.*

HURGADA

Coral Beach Hotel (065)442160/1/2.
El-Giftun Village (065)442667
Hotel Inter Continental (065)443911 - fax (065)443910.
Jasmine Village (065)442442 - fax (065)442441.
Magawish Village (065)442620 - fax (065)442759.
Mashrabia Village (065)443330 - fax (065)443344.
Moon Valley Hotel (065)442811.
Paradiso Resort (065)447935/6/7.
Princess Hotel (065)443100/1/2.
Sheraton Hotel (065)442000 - fax (065)442033.

Sonesta Resort
(065)443660/1 - fax
(065)443661.
Westin Resort
(065)443240/1/2.

EL-ARISH

Oberoi (068)351321.

ST. CATHERINE

Daniela Village
(062)7497732.
Monastery 770945.
St. Catherine Village
(062)770456 - fax
(062)720221.

DIVING CENTER

SHARM EL-SHEIKH

African Divers
(062)600307, Ras Um
Sid Dive Site.
Aquamarine Diving Center
(062)600276 - fax
(062)600176.
Aquanaute Diving Center
(062)600187 - fax
(062)600619, Naama
Bay.
Aquavision by Venus
(062)600280.
Camel Diving College
(062)600700 - fax
(062)600601 Naama
Bay.
Colona Dive Club
(062)600184/5 - fax
(062)600185, Naama
Bay.
Diving Center
(062)600276 - fax
(062)600176, Naama
Bay.
Divers'Den (062)600195
Divers'Lodge (2)3453552
(Cairo) - fax
(2)3027383, Naama
Bay.
Embarak Diving Resorts
(062)600942 - fax
(062)600944, Shark
Bay.
New Tiran Diving Center
(062)600225 - fax
(062)600220, Naama
Bay.
Ocean Quest Plc
(062)600268 - fax
(2)770726, Sharm el-
Maya.
Oonas Divers
(062)600581 - fax
(062)600582, Naama
Bay.

Red Sea Diving College
(062)600145/4 - fax
(062)600144, Naama
Bay.
Red Sea Diving Club
(062)600343 -·fax
(062)600342, Naama
Bay.
Scubatour (062)600167
(062)600166, Sharm el-
Maya.
Shark Bay
(062)600942/3.
Sinai Divers
(062)600697-
(062)600150/1 - fax
(062)600158-600155,
Naama Bay.
Sinai Dive Club (2)760575
(Cairo) -
(062)600140(Sinai) -
fax (2)770726.
Subex Diving Center
(062)600100/5 - fax
(062)600111, Naama
Bay.
Sultana Dive Center
(062)600144.
Tentoria Diving Center
(062)600350 - fax
(062)600334, Sharm el-
Maya; (062)600280/1 -
fax (062)600282,
Naama Bay.
Tiran Dive club
(062)600285, Naama
Bay.

DAHAB

Canyon Dive Club
(062)640043, Canyon
Dive Site.
Dahab Dive Center
(062)770788 - fax
(062)776736, PLM Azur
Hotel.
Fantasea Divers
(062)640043, Assalah
Village.
INMO (062)640370/1 -
fax (062)640372, el-
Mashraba.
Jugo Riepl (062))640093.
Nesima Diving Center
(062)640320 - fax
(062)640321, el-
Mashraba.
Sinai Dive Club
(062)640302, PLM Azur
Hotel.

NUWEIBA

Aqua Sport (062)520320
- fax (062)520327.

TABA

Taba Hilton Diving Center
(062)771888 - fax
(062)771461, Taba
Hilton.

HURGADA

Aquanut Red SGA. Diving
Guide (065)447045.
Coral Beach Hotel
(065)442160/1/2.
James & Mac
(065)442665/7/8 - fax
(065)442666-442300.
Paradiso Resort
(065)447935/6/7.
Simbad (065)443261/6 -
fax (065)447471.
Sonesta Resort
(065)443660/1.
Subex (065))447593 - fax
(065)447471.
Westin Resort
(065)44324/1/2.

TRAVEL AGENTS

SHARM EL-SHEIKH

Alpitour (062)600911/2,
Naama Bay.
Best Tour (062)600857/8,
Sharm Mall-Naama.
Clipper (062)600280.
Egypt Travel
(062)600164.
Emeco (062)600266,
Hilton Residence.
Franco Rosso
(062)600591, Naama
Bay (New Tiran Hotel).
Inter Egypt
(062)600591/2, Naama
Bay (New Tiran Hotel).
Ita Tours (062)600140,
Hilton Fayouz Hotel-
Naama.
Jet Arrow (062)601777 -
fax (062)600250, Sharm
Mall-Naama.
Misr Sinai Touristic Co.
(062)600640, Sharm el-
Maya.
National Travel Service
(062)600911/2, Naama
Bay (New Tiran Hotel).
Pianeta Terra
(062)600150-600685,
Naama Bay (New Tiran
Hotel).
Safaga Travel
(062)600185/6.
Scubatour (062)600166.
Seti First Travel
(062)600378, Seti
Sharm Hotel.

Siag Travel (062)600860-
600893/4/5 - fax
(062)600201, Naama
Bay (New Tiran Hotel).
South Sinai Travel
(062)600150/69,
Ghazala Hotel.
Spring Tours
(062)600130/1/2, Tiran
Village.
Starco Travel
(062)601300, New Tiran
Hotel.
Tips (062)600208,
Sanafir.
Tiran Tours
(062)600221/2, Tiran
Village.
Top Team Service
(062)600961 - fax
(062)600962, Sharm
Mall-Naama.
Trans Egypt (062)600127,
Naama Bay (Tiran
Village).
Travco (062)600764,
Naama Bay (Mövenpick
Jolie Ville).
Turisanda (062)600127 -
fax (062)600129,
Naama Bay.
Viaggi del Ventaglio
(062)600186, Sharm
Club.

CAR RENTAL

SHARM EL-SHEIKH

Europcar-Max
(062)600686, Fayrouz
Hilton.
Europcar-Max (2)771284,
Ghazala Hotel.
Hertz (062)600459,
Naama Bay.
Siag Travel
(062)600893/4/5.
Top Team Service
(062)600961 - fax
(062)600962, Sharm
Mall-Naama.

TABA

Europcar-Max (2)763544,
Taba Hilton.

MEDICAL CENTER

SHARM EL-SHEIKH

Hyperbaric Service
(062)600922/3
(062)601011.

INDEX OF LOCALITIES

A

Abu Aweigila: 16, 25.
Abu Galum: 108, 109.
Abu Gifa: 146.
Abu Rudeis: 28.
Abu Seifa: 22.
Abu Sheib: 36.
Abu Suweira: 27
Abu Zenima: 17, 28, 31, 36, 40.
Africa: 47.
A.H. tunnel of: 22, 25, 40.
Ahmed Hamdi tunnel of: 26, 101, 113, 114.
Ain Furtaga: 112, 113, 114, 118.
Ain Kid: 76, 77.
Ain Khudra: 100, 104, 105, 112, 113, 118.
Ain Naghila: 146, 147.
Ain Qudeirat: 25.
Ain Umm Ahmed: 113, 118.
Amphoras: 68.
Anemone City: 54.
Amphitheater of the Seventy Wise Man of Israel: 138.
Aqaba: 16, 51, 82, 94, 99.
Aqaba Beach: 51
Aqaba Beach, gulf of: 6, 12, 13, 17, 25, 26, 29, 44, 76, 80, 86, 108, 138.
Ayun Musa: 26, 27.

B

Balouza: 22, 23.
Bardawil: 10, 23, 24.
Basata: 101.
Basilica of the Transfiguration: 123.
Bawaki Hotel: 101.
Beacon Rock: 52.
Bir el-Abd: 16, 24, 25.
Bir el-Shenar: 150.
Bir Gifgata: 16, 25.
Bir Nasib: 9, 36.
Bitter lakes: 16, 20, 23.
Blue Desert: 89, 121, 152.
Blue Hole: 86, 96, 99.
Bubasti: 20.

C

Canaan: 25.
Canyon: 86, 96, 99.
Caves: 98.
Chapel of the Burning Bush: 129.
Chapel of the Golden Calf: 120.
Club Aquasun: 101.
Colored Canyon: 113, 114.
Coral Bay: 61.
Coral Island: 101.
Costantinople: 21.
Crete: 123.

D

Dagashland: 27.
Dahab: 61, 81, 86, 89, 91, 92, 94, 96, 98, 99, 100, 101, 104, 120, 121.
Deir: 121.
Deir el-Arbain: 121, 150.
Deir el-Rahab: 146.
Deir el-Ribwa: 146, 150.
Devil's Head: 101.
Diwar Dvawara: 122.
Dolphin Beach Hotel: 101.

E

Easter Desert: 17.
Egypt: 6, 10, 12, 21, 23, 79, 123, 152.
Eilat: 10.
El-Arish: 17, 22, 23, 24, 25.
El-Bueib: 39.
El-Ferdan: 21.
El-Gardeb: 51, 54, 99.
El-Guels: 23.
Elin: 29.
El-Karghana: 80.
El-Kuntilla, oase of: 16.
El Markha: 28, 40.
El-Qantara: 21, 24.
El-Qantara Gharb: 22.
El-Qantara Sharq: 22.
El Quseima: 16, 25.
El-Raha: 120, 121, 122.
El-Sayaddin: 13.
El-Tor: 17, 26, 29, 38, 40, 72.
Ezion Gaber: 10.

F

Far Garden: 68.
Farsh Rumanna: 148.
Feiran: 39, 41, 121.
Feiran, oase of: 38.
Fjord: 101.

G

Galbana: 22.
Galt: 148.
Galt el-Azraq: 146, 148.
Gate of Confession: 138.
Gate of Saint Stephen: 138.
Gebel Abbas: 146.
Gebel Katherina: 6, 121, 123, 146, 150.
Gebel Dagilat: 72.
Gebel el-Deir: 120.
Gebel Freiah: 39.
Gebel Fuga: 40, 41.
Gebel Ghorabi: 32.
Gebel Halal: 10, 16.
Gebel Hamman Musa: 29.
Gebel Horeb: 122, 138.
Gebel Igma: 16.
Gebel Maghara: 6, 7, 16, 17, 25, 40.
Gebel Marahil: 37.
Gebel Matalla: 31.
Gebel Megafa: 121.
Gebel Meharret: 38, 39.
Gebel Milehes: 112.
Gebel Misman: 146.
Gebel Musa: 6, 10, 25, 120, 121, 122, 138, 141, 150.
Gebel Nabq Baharia: 148.
Gebel Raha: 16.
Gebel Rahab: 146.
Gebel Ruwesat el-Nima: 72.
Gebel Serabit el-Khadem: 32.
Gebel Seru: 146.
Gebel Sinai: 10.
Gebel Sukhn: 109.
Gebel Tahuna: 39.
Gebel Tarbush: 148.
Gebel Zebir: 150.
Gerrah, port of: 24.
Ghazala: 91.
Gorah: 13.

Gordon Reef: 82.
Green Lodge: 121.

H

Hamman Faraun Malun: 27.
Hamman Musa: 29.
Haggar Maktub: 104.
Hedjaz: 17.
Hesi el-Khatiatin: 38.
Hidden Bay: 44, 49, 50, 54.
Highland of el-Tih: 7.
Holiday Village: 98.
Holy Mountain: 120.
Holy Land: 23.
Horus, track of: 22.
Hurghada: 61.

I

Ismailia: 16, 21, 25.
Israel: 14, 79, 101, 152.

J

Jackson Reef: 82.
Jericho: 10.
Jerusalem: 39, 123.
Jethro: 28.
Jordan: 14, 17.

K

Kadesh-Bernea: 10.
Kasserwit: 24.
Khatmia: 25.
Khessuam, oase of: 38.

L

Lake Timsah: 20, 23.
Lighthouse: 98.

M

Maghara: 28, 40.
Main Beach: 51.
Mangroves, channel of: 44, 49.
Mangroves, island of: 44, 49.
Mangroves, oase of: 78.
Manzala: 10.
Markha: 40.
Marsa Bareka: 48, 55.
Marsa el-Aat: 72.

Marsa el-Muqabila: 101.
Marsa Ghazlani: 48.
Mecca: 20, 26.
Mediterranean sea: 6, 20, 21, 22, 23.
Melga: 120, 121, 150.
Merneptah: 10.
Migdol, fortress of: 22.
Mohammedia: 24.
Mons Kasios: 23.
Mövenpick: 72.
Mudjan: 10.
Mushroom: 52.

N

Naama Bay: 61, 68, 72, 73, 86.
Nabq: 76, 78, 79.
Nabq, parc of: 47.
Nabq Zawatin: 146.
Nakhl: 14, 16, 25, 26.
Nakhlet el-Tel: 80.
Nasb, oase of: 86, 88, 108.
Nawamis: 105.
Near Garden: 68.
New Qantara Sharq: 22.
Nile: 6, 20.
Nile Delta: 23.
Nuweiba: 17, 25, 26, 39, 89, 94, 96, 99, 100, 101, 104, 109, 112, 113, 114, 120, 121.
Nuweiba Holiday Village: 101.
Nuweiba Muzeina: 101.

P

Palestine: 17, 23, 123.
Pelousion: 22.
Pelusium: 23, 31.
Peremun: 23.
Petra in Jordan: 113.
Pharao's Island: 101.
Pi-Ramesses (or Pitom): 10.
Port Fuad: 21.
Port Said: 21.
Promise Land: 6.

Q

Qadesh-Barnea: 25.
Qalaat el-Qundi: 27.
Quay el-Qundi: 27.
Quay: 49, 52.
Qura: 91.

R

Rafah: 22, 25
Rafia: 25.
Ramlet Himeiyr: 41.
Ras Abu Galum: 96, 100.
Ras Atar: 55.
Ras el-Burqa: 101.
Ras el-Qelb: 118.
Ras Ghazlani: 55.
Ras Malaab: 27.
Ras Materma: 27.
Ras Mohammed: 26, 29, 43, 44, 45, 46, 47, 48, 52, 56, 78, 80, 82, 108.
Ras Nasrani: 61, 68, 69, 79, 86.
Ras Safsafa: 120, 121, 138.
Ras Sudr: 27.
Ras Umm Sidd: 61, 68.
Red Sea: 6, 10, 17, 20, 21, 23, 26, 27, 44, 46, 78, 86.
Reithou: 29.
Rest Valley Mountain: 86, 94.
Ribwa: 121.
Rumana: 23, 24.

S

Saint Catherine, village of: 8, 26, 28, 29, 38, 41, 89, 100, 104, 105, 109, 113, 120, 121, 123, 138.
Saint Catherine, monastery of: 6, 17, 38, 39, 121, 122, 146, 152.
Saint Galatio: 121.
Saint Helene, church of: 123.
Saint Theodore: 121.
Sally Land Tourist Village: 101.
Saudi Arabia: 82, 94.
Sayaddin Beach Hotel: 101.
Sebayat el-Deir: 18
Serabit: 28, 31, 40, 41.
Serabit el-Khadem: 8, 9, 28, 32, 34, 36, 38, 41.
Shaab Ali: 52.
Shag Rock: 52.
Sharira: 86, 92.
Shark Bay: 61, 68, 81, 86.
Shark Observatory Bay: 44, 45, 51, 54.

Shark Reef: 54.
Sharm: 61, 81, 82, 89, 94, 99.
Sharm Dahab: 75.
Sharm el-Maiya: 29, 61.
Sharm el-Sheikh: 13, 26, 29, 38, 43, 56, 61, 68, 73, 81, 86, 91, 94.
Sharm Mall: 72.
Shaqq Musa: 150.
Sheikh Abu Sheib: 39.
Sheikh Coast: 61, 73, 86.
Sheikh Habus: 41.
Sheikh Hamid: 41.
Sheikh Harun: 120.
Sheikh Musa Mountain: 150.
Sheikh Nabi Salam: 39, 120, 152.
Sheikh Soliman: 40.
Sheikh Zuweid: 25.
Sikket el-Basha: 138, 141.
Sikket Saydna Musa: 138, 141.
Sin: 6.
Sinai: 6, 7, 8, 10, 12, 14, 16, 17, 19, 20, 21, 22, 23, 25 26, 29, 31, 39, 40, 43, 47, 49, 61, 78, 79, 80, 91, 105, 113, 118, 122, 123, 150.
Small Crack: 52.
Southern Oasis: 98.
Split Rock: 73.
Sudr Beach Hotel: 27.
Suez: 20, 21, 25.
Suez Beach: 49.
Suez, channel of: 16, 21, 22, 26, 29, 38, 44, 48, 120.
Sun Pool: 101.
Syria: 14, 25.

T

Taba: 100, 101, 113.
Taiyba: 28.
Tamad: 16.
Tarabin: 101.
Tarfat: 39.
Tcharu: 24.
Tell Abu Seifa: 22.
Tell el-Farama: 22, 23.
Tell Hebua: 24.
Tell el-Herr: 22.
Tell el-Makhazna: 23.
Temple: 62.
Thistlegorm: 52.

Thomas Reef: 82.
Timna (I, II): 8.
Timsah: 8.
Tiran, island of: 82.
Tiran, strait of: 12, 13, 21, 69, 79, 82.

U

Umm Bogma: 37.

W

Wadi Abu Gifa: 146.
Wadi-Ahmar: 8.
Wadi Baba: 37, 40.
Wadi Bata: 32.
Wadi Budra: 40.
Wadi Connection: 86, 94.
Wadi Dhaba: 32.
Wadi Disco: 112.
Wadi el-Aat: 72.
Wadi el-Aat Sharqui; 72.
Wadi el-Ain: 118, 119
Wadi el-Akhdar: 39, 41.
Wadi el-Deir: 120, 121, 138, 150.
Wadi el-Lega: 120, 121, 150.
Wadi el-Sheikh: 120.
Wadi el-Tor: 29.
Wadi Feiran: 26, 29, 38, 40, 120.
Wadi Gharandal: 27.
Wadi Gharvel: 38.
Wadi Ghazala: 104. 112, 113.
Wadi Iqna: 40.
Wadi Jethro: 120.
Wadi Jibal: 146, 148.
Wadi Khabila: 81.
Wadi Khamila: 41.
Wadi Kharig: 9, 36, 37, 40.
Wadi Khresa: 81.
Wadi Khudra: 105, 118.
Wadi Kid: 76, 81, 88.
Wadi Labwa: 41.
Wadi Lethi: 118.
Wadi Madsus. 86, 88.
Wadi Maghara: 8, 28, 38, 40, 41.
Wadi Mandar: 75.
Wadi Matalla: 28, 31.
Wadi Mikeimin: 118.
Wadi Mukattab: 38, 40.
Wadi Nasb: 88, 89.
Wadi Nash: 86.
Wadi Nasib: 31, 34, 36, 37.

Wadi Nekheil: 114.
Wadi Qabila: 78: 78.
Wadi Qenaia: 40.
Wadi Qnai el-Atshan: 92, 94.
Wadi Qnai el-Rayan: 86: 92.
Wadi Saada: 100, 112.
Wadi Samghi: 112.
Wadi Sarbout: 32.
Wadi Sawik: 32.
Wadi Shaq: 146.
Wadi Sheikh: 41.
Wadi Shellal: 37, 86, 88, 89.

Wadi Shetan: 86, 88, 89.
Wadi Shoeib: 120.
Wadi Sidri: 28, 40, 41.
Wadi Talah: 146, 148.
Wadi Tayiba: 27.
Wadi Tubuq: 146.
Wadi Tumilath: 20.
Wadi Umm Misma: 94.
Wadi Wardan: 27.
Wadi Watir: 101, 113.
Wadi Zawatin: 146.
Watia: 39.

Wichita Falls: 86.
Woodhouse: 82.

Y

Yolanda Bay: 51.
Yolanda Reef: 54.

Z

Zaranik: 24.

MAPS SYMBOLS

- ● Diving site
- ⬤ Town
- ▲ Mountain
- ☦ Christian place of worship
- ☪ Muslim place of worship
- ♀ Lighthouse
- ⚒ Mining site

- ■P Parking area
- ✈ Airport
- — · — Border
- ▬▬ Main road
- ──── Secondary road
- - - - - Trail

NB - In the maps, unless specifically indicated, the "North" facing upward.

PHOTOGRAPHIC CREDITS

Marcello Bertinetti/Archivio White Star: pages 15 bottom, 28 center left, 28 bottom left, 29, 39 bottom, 45 bottom right, 46 bottom, 52 bottom, 54 bottom, 58 center, 62 bottom, 63, 65 bottom, 67 center, 70 center, 83 center right, 83 bottom right, 84 center right, 84 bottom right, 84 bottom left, 93 bottom, 97 top, 99 bottom, 102 top right, 102 bottom, 104, 122, 123 top, 123 bottom, 124-125, 128 center, 128 bottom, 130 top left, 136 bottom, 137 bottom left, 138, 145 top.

Franco Banfi: pages 47 top left, 57 top left.

Duba: pages 53 bottom left, 55 top right, 57 center right, 82 top, 85 top, 97 center right, 137 bottom right.

Edotike: pages 134, 135.

Andrea and Antonella Ferrari: pages 47 bottom, 71 bottom left.

Paolo Fossati: pages 55 bottom right, 70 top, 99 center left.

Itamar Grinberg: pages 56 bottom, 99 top.

Italo Monetti: pages 116, 117 top and center left, 117 bottom.

Alberto Muro Pelliconi: pages 47 top right, 71 top left, 96 bottom, 97 center left.

NASA: pages 4-5, 6.

Vincenzo Paolillo: pages 69 bottom, 99 center right.

Sergio Quaglia: page 71 bottom right.

Roberto Rinaldi: pages 52 center, 53 top, 53 center right, 53 bottom right, 55 top left, 55 bottom left, 55 center right, 56 top, 57 top right, 58 top, 58 bottom, 59, 68 center, 69 center right, 70 bottom, 85 center, 85 bottom.

Jeff Rotman: pages 57 bottom, 71 top right, 83 bottom, 97 bottom.

Alberto Siliotti/Archivio C.D.A.: pages 1, 7, 8, 9, 10, 11, 12, 13, 14, 15, 16, 17, 18, 19, 20, 21, 22, 23, 24, 25, 26, 27, 28 top right, 28 top left, 30, 32, 33, 34, 35, 36, 37, 39 top, 39 center, 40, 41, 42, 43, 44, 45 top, 45 center, 45 bottom left, 46 top, 46 center, 48, 49, 50, 51, 52 top, 54 top, 60, 61, 62 top, 62 center, 65 top left, 65 top right, 66, 67 top, 67 bottom, 68 top, 68 bottom, 69 top, 72, 73, 75, 76, 77, 78, 79, 80, 81, 82 bottom, 83 top, 84 top, 86, 87, 88, 89, 91, 92, 93 top, 93 center, 94, 95, 96 top, 96 center, 98, 101, 102 top left, 102 center left, 102 center right, 105, 106, 107, 108, 109, 110-111, 113, 114, 117 top right, 118, 119, 120, 121, 123 center, 128 top, 129, 130, 131, 132-133, 136 top, 137 top and center, 141, 142-143, 145 center, 145 bottom, 147, 148, 149, 150, 151, 152, 153, 160.

Alberto Vanzo : page 84 center left.

Claudio Ziraldo: pages 47 center, 69 center left, 83 top left.

159